BASIC REAL ESTATE
SECRETS
THEY DON'T WANT
YOU TO KNOW

ALBERTO MOLINA

Basic Real Estate Secrets They Don't Want You To Know

By Alberto Molina

Privacy Policy and Earnings Disclaimer

This book is sold with the understanding that neither the publisher nor the Authors are engaged in rendering legal investment or accounting information, nor are they offering professional services. If legal advice or expert assistance is required the services of a competent professional should be sought out when necessary. The information ideas and suggestions contained herein have been developed from sources including publications and research that are considered and believed to be reliable but cannot be guaranteed.

The author specifically disclaim any liability or risk personal or otherwise incurred as consequence directly or indirectly of the use and application of any of the techniques or contents of this book.

Contents

Dedication

I Dedicate this book to YOU, for reading it and taking action. You don't have to be rich or powerful to know these secrets.

What This Book Will Do For You

Welcome to The Basic Real Estate Secrets They Don't Want You To Know. If you're reading this book, chances are you're tired of living a life that feels like it's stuck in neutral.

You're tired of working hard but not seeing the results you want. You're tired of feeling like you're always one paycheck away from financial disaster. You're tired of feeling like there's more to life, but you don't know how to get there.

Well, I'm here to tell you that there is more to life, and it's not as complicated as you might think. In this book, I'm going to share with you the basic secrets that the rich and successful don't want you to know. These are the secrets that can help you take control of your financial future, achieve your goals, and live the life you've always wanted.

Now, you might be thinking, Why would the rich and successful keep secrets from me? The truth is, they're not doing it to be mean or selfish. It's just that they've learned these secrets through trial and error, and they don't want to share them because they're afraid of losing their advantage.

But I'm here to tell you that you don't have to be rich or powerful to know these secrets. You just have to be willing to learn and apply them.

In this book, I'll be sharing with you the principles that have helped me achieve freedom in my own life. I'll be drawing on my own experiences, as well as the experiences of other successful and incredible people I've met along the way.

I'll be showing you how you can think differently about money, how you can manage your finances, and how you can build wealth over time.

But before we dive into the secrets themselves, let me tell you a little bit about my own story.

Introduction

I grew up in a Hispanic working class family, and like most people, I was taught to go to school, get good grades, and find a good job. And that's exactly what I did. I started working long hours, but I wasn't getting ahead financially.

I was living paycheck to paycheck, and I felt like I always had more month at the end of the month, than money at the end of the month. I realized that no matter how hard I worked, I was never going to get ahead if I kept doing what I was doing.

So, I started reading books and attending local real estate seminars. I learned about the power of using "OPM" other people's money, "OPE" other people's experience, and "OPT" other people's time, and I started investing in real estate.

It wasn't easy, and I made some mistakes along the way, but over time, I started to see results.

I was able to live a life that I never thought was possible.

And that's one of the reason that inspired me to write this book. I want to share with you the basic secrets that helped me achieve freedom from the 9 to 5 system. I want to show you that you don't have to be rich or powerful to live the life you've always wanted. All you need is the right mindset, be coachable, teachable, and ready to take action.

Growing up in a Hispanic working class family, I was no stranger to financial struggles. My mother worked tirelessly to provide for us, but it always seemed like there was never enough money to go around. I remember watching my mom worry about paying bills, making ends meet, and planning for an uncertain future. This environment taught me the value of hard work, but it also made me question if there was a better way to achieve financial stability.

As I got older, I began searching for answers to break the cycle of financial hardship and provide a better life for my family. My quest for knowledge led me to the world of real estate investing, which proved to be a life changing discovery. Through countless hours of research, networking, and hands on experience, I learned the ins and outs of the industry and, more importantly, uncovered the secrets that many successful investors don't want you to know.

I am sharing my story and the knowledge I've gained along the way in this book, "BASIC REAL ESTATE SECRETS THEY DON'T WANT YOU TO KNOW". My hope is that by sharing my journey, I can help others from similar backgrounds realize that achieving freedom through real estate investing is possible. It doesn't matter where you come from or what your current financial situation is, with the right mindset, education, and determination, anyone can build a prosperous future through real estate.

In the chapters that follow, We will explore various investment strategies, delve into the art of negotiation, and discuss the importance of building a reliable team. Along the way, I will also share my own experiences.

This book is more than just a collection of real estate secrets, it is an invitation to embark on a journey of personal and financial transformation. The Basic Secrets They Don't Want You To Know is a book that can help you achieve freedom and success over time.

If you're ready to take control of your financial future, if you're ready to live the life you've always wanted, then this book is for you.

Welcome aboard the journey.

Your friend,
Alberto Molina.

Chapter 1

Building a Solid Foundation

As a child, I remember my mother sharing a story that has always stuck with me, and as I ventured into the world of real estate investing, I realized just how valuable that lesson truly was. The story goes like this.

Once upon a time, in a small village, two men decided to build their homes. The first man chose to build his house on a rocky cliff overlooking the ocean, while the second man chose to build his house on the sandy shore near the water. Both men worked diligently, constructing their homes with care and precision. However, when the first storm arrived, the man who built his house on the sand found that his home was swept away by the relentless waves. The man who built his house on the rock, however, saw his home stand firm against the wind and rain.

The lesson my mother taught me through this story is that the foundation upon which we build our lives is crucial to our success. In the world of real estate investing, this lesson couldn't be more relevant. As a real estate investor, building a solid foundation is the first secret they don't want you to know.

In this book, I will be sharing with you the secrets that have helped me succeed in the world of real estate investing. The first step is to establish a strong foundation upon which you can build your business. This means understanding your goals, your resources, and your limitations. It also means educating yourself about the market, the various types of investments available, and the strategies that have proven successful for others.

One of the most important aspects of building a solid foundation is understanding your "why." Your "why" is the driving force behind your actions, the reason you are willing to take risks, and the motivation that keeps you pushing forward even when the going gets tough. For me, my "why" was to create financial freedom for my family, and to have the ability to give back to my community. By defining your "why," you can maintain focus and stay committed to your goals.

Another essential aspect of building a solid foundation is continuously seeking knowledge. The real estate industry is constantly evolving, and it's crucial to stay informed and educated about the latest trends, strategies, and opportunities. Read books, attend seminars, and network with other investors. By doing so, you'll not only strengthen your foundation but also be better equipped to make informed decisions and capitalize on opportunities as they arise.

One of the most crucial component of a solid foundation is your mindset. Real estate investing is not for the faint of heart. There will be challenges, obstacles, and setbacks along the way. Developing a resilient and adaptable mindset will help you navigate these challenges and ensure your long-term success.

Remember, the first secret they don't want you to know about real estate investing is building a solid foundation. By focusing on your "why," continuously seeking knowledge, and developing a strong mindset, you'll be well on your way to creating a thriving and successful real estate investing business.

As you embark on this journey, I encourage you to keep my mother's story in mind. Just like the man who built his house on the rock, a solid foundation will enable you to weather the storms and come out stronger on the other side. Let this be the first of many lessons I share with you as we explore the 48 chapters of "Basic Real Estate Secrets They Don't Want You to Know."

In the coming chapters, I will share with you some of the most crucial lessons I've learned throughout my years as a real estate investor, lessons that have not only helped me build my own empire but also helped countless others who have followed in my footsteps. By sharing these secrets, I hope to empower you with the tools and knowledge necessary to build your own solid foundation in the world of real estate investing.

One of the most important aspects of building a solid foundation is understanding the importance of constant learning and self improvement. Just like any other field, real estate investing is continually evolving, and it's crucial to stay up to date with the latest trends, strategies, and technologies. By doing so, you'll be better equipped to adapt to changing market conditions and seize new opportunities as they arise.

Another key element of a solid foundation is the cultivation of strong relationships with other professionals in the industry. Surrounding yourself with like minded individuals who share your passion for real estate investing will not only provide you with valuable insights and advice but also foster an environment of mutual support and collaboration.

As we embark on this journey together, I encourage you to remain open minded, committed, and determined. With the right foundation in place, there's no limit to what you can achieve in the world of real estate investing.

Chapter 2

The Real Estate Mindset

Years ago, I was invited to a neighborhood barbecue where I met a wise old man named Juan. I discovered that he was a seasoned real estate investor with an impressive property portfolio. But what struck me the most about Juan was his mindset and attitude towards real estate investing. As we sipped on cold beverages and enjoyed the aroma of sizzling steaks, Juan shared with me invaluable insights that would change my approach to real estate investing forever.

Juan emphasized that the real estate mindset is one of the first and most important secrets to success in this industry. It goes beyond motivational talk and positive affirmations. It's an unwavering commitment to do whatever it takes, at any time, for anyone you love. This same mindset, he explained, is what has driven him to excel in the world of real estate investing.

He shared a story about a time when he encountered a distressed seller who needed to sell her property quickly due to a family emergency. Rather than taking advantage of the situation for his own benefit, Juan's mindset guided him to help the seller get the best possible outcome. He connected her with other investors in his network and ensured that she received a fair price for her property. Juan's actions were a testament to the importance of the real estate mindset in action.

Juan also emphasized that a strong real estate mindset enables you to see opportunities where others might see only obstacles. He recalled an instance when he purchased a dilapidated property that no one else wanted. While others saw a money pit, Juan saw the potential for profit. With determination and hard work, he transformed the rundown house into a beautiful home, ultimately selling it for a significant profit. This ability to recognize opportunities is a key aspect of the real estate mindset.

One evening, Juan invited me to join him on a tour of his properties. As we walked through each building, he pointed out the various improvements he had made and the challenges he had faced along the way. What struck me was Juan's unwavering belief in his ability to overcome any obstacle and his relentless pursuit of success. This, he explained, was the essence of the real estate mindset, the ability to push through adversity and never give up on your goals.

As the sun began to set and the barbecue started winding down, Juan shared one last piece of wisdom. He told me that the real estate mindset is not something that can be learned overnight, but rather, it's something that must be cultivated and nurtured over time. He suggested that I read books, attend seminars, and surround myself with like minded individuals to help develop and maintain this mindset.

Juan's insights that day provided me with a new perspective on real estate investing. The real estate mindset is not just about thinking positively or being motivated, it's about making decisions rooted in love and dedication, overcoming challenges, and recognizing opportunities. With this mindset, you'll be well equipped to embark on a successful journey in the world of real estate investing.

As you continue to read "Basic Real Estate Secrets They Don't Want You to Know," I hope that Juan's story inspires you to develop and maintain your own real estate mindset. Embrace this essential secret to success, and you'll be well on your way to unlocking the true potential of real estate investing. Let Juan's wisdom guide you as you navigate the challenges and opportunities that await you in this exciting and rewarding industry.

By embracing the real estate mindset, you'll be well equipped to navigate the ups and downs of the industry and ultimately achieve the success you desire. With this foundation, you can confidently continue your journey through "Basic Real Estate Secrets They Don't Want You to

Know," applying the principles and lessons you learn to your own real estate investing endeavors.

Let the wisdom and experiences shared in this chapter serve as a beacon of inspiration as you forge ahead, ready to unlock the full potential of real estate investing. And always remember the importance of maintaining your real estate mindset, for it is truly one of the most powerful secrets to achieving greatness in this exciting and rewarding field.

Chapter 3

Understanding Real Estate Markets

One warm afternoon, I found myself chatting with my friend and fellow real estate investor, Carlos, who had an uncanny ability to identify profitable deals before anyone else in town. His exceptional decision-making skills always intrigued me, and I couldn't resist asking him for advice on how to get started in real estate investing.

Carlos invited me to join him for a walk along the famous River Walk in San Antonio, where we could discuss his strategies and insights in a relaxed atmosphere. As we strolled along the winding path, admiring the lush greenery, quaint shops, and bustling restaurants, he shared a story that would forever change my perspective on real estate investing. He told me about two friends, Ruben and Lalo, who were both looking to invest in real estate. Ruben had a keen understanding of the local real estate market, while Lalo was just getting started and lacked the same level of knowledge.

Ruben and Lalo both came across a potential investment property in a rapidly growing neighborhood. The property had great potential, but it was in need of significant repairs. Ruben, being familiar with the local market, quickly analyzed the situation and determined that the cost of repairs would be well worth it, given the potential return on investment. He made an offer on the property and secured the deal.

On the other hand, Lalo hesitated. He wasn't sure if the neighborhood's growth would continue or if the property would be a wise investment after factoring in the repair costs. Ultimately, Lalo decided not to make an offer, and he missed out on the opportunity.

As time went by, the neighborhood continued to flourish, and property values soared. Ruben's investment paid off handsomely, while Lalo was left to wonder what might have been. Carlos emphasized that it was Ruben's understanding of the local market that gave him the confidence to take advantage of the opportunity, while Lalo's uncertainty held him back.

As I listened intently to Carlos, he continued to share invaluable advice about understanding real estate markets. He explained that it's crucial to be aware of the dynamics that drive market changes, such as supply and demand, interest rates, and government policies. These factors can have a significant impact on property values and investment opportunities.

Carlos also emphasized the importance of analyzing various market indicators, including median home prices, rental rates, vacancy rates, and days on the market. By monitoring these indicators, investors can gain a comprehensive understanding of the health of the real estate market and make informed decisions.

He suggested that I familiarize myself with the concept of "sub-markets" - specific areas within a city or region that can have their own unique market dynamics. By understanding the intricacies of these sub-markets, investors can more accurately assess investment opportunities and make better decisions.

Carlos shared a personal story of a time when he noticed an emerging trend in one of San Antonio's sub-markets. He observed that an increasing number of young professionals were moving into the area due to an influx of new job opportunities. Recognizing the potential for growth, Carlos capitalized on this trend by purchasing several rental properties in the neighborhood. As more young professionals moved in, the demand for housing increased, resulting in higher rental rates and property values.

Carlos' keen understanding of the sub-market allowed him to stay ahead of the competition and profit significantly from his investments. He explained that this was a prime example of the power of understanding real estate markets and being proactive in identifying opportunities.

During our walk, Carlos also discussed the value of building a network of industry professionals, such as real estate agents, property managers, and fellow investors. These connections can provide invaluable insights and advice on local market trends, helping investors stay informed and make better decisions.

As we concluded our walk along the River Walk, I couldn't help but feel grateful for the wisdom Carlos had shared with me. It was clear that understanding real estate markets was one of the secrets they don't want you to know about because it's how they stay ahead of the competition. By developing a deep understanding of market dynamics and staying informed about local trends, new real estate investors can be more successful than those who don't know this crucial secret.

As we parted ways, I thanked Carlos for his invaluable insights and promised to put them into practice.

So, as you continue to explore the secrets they don't want you to know in this book, remember that a deep understanding of real estate markets is a powerful tool in your arsenal. Embrace the knowledge, stay informed, and use it to your advantage as you build a thriving and successful real estate investing business.

Chapter 4

The Art of the Hunt

In my early days of real estate investing, I spent countless hours studying various strategies and learning from them. One day, as I was sitting in my office, I received a call from an old friend, José. He was a seasoned real estate investor who had an uncanny ability to find great deals. I admired his tenacity and his knack for uncovering hidden gems. As we talked, José mentioned something that struck a chord with me. He said, "Alberto, real estate investing is like going hunting. The prize is the perfect property."

At first, I was puzzled by his analogy. However, as I started to reflect on my experiences, I realized he was right. Hunting for the ideal property is an art form in itself. It requires patience, persistence, and a keen eye for detail. The art of the hunt is one of the first real estate secrets they don't want you to know. In this chapter, I will share my personal stories and insights to help you become a master hunter in the world of real estate.

When I started my journey in real estate, I used to spend hours driving around neighborhoods, looking for properties that seemed undervalued or had potential. I would take notes, research the properties, and try to find the best deals. One day, while driving through a familiar neighborhood, I spotted a small, run-down house. The exterior was in disrepair, and the overgrown yard indicated it had been neglected for some time. I saw potential in this property and decided to dig deeper.

After conducting my research, I discovered the property was owned by an elderly woman who had recently passed away. Her children, who lived out of state, were eager to sell the house and be done with it. They had little interest in making repairs and simply wanted to cash out as quickly as possible. I seized the opportunity and negotiated a price far below market value. After some minor renovations, I was able to flip the property for a healthy profit. This experience taught me the value of patience and persistence in the hunt for the perfect property.

As I continued my real estate journey, I came across a unique opportunity that truly tested my hunting skills. I had heard whispers in the investor community about a large commercial property that had been sitting vacant for some time. The previous owner had gone bankrupt, and the bank was eager to sell the property. Intrigued, I decided to investigate further.

The property was a 20-unit apartment complex, located on the outskirts of town. It had been built in the 1970s and was in desperate need of renovation. The neighborhood surrounding the complex had seen better days, but there were signs of revitalization and growth. I recognized the potential for a significant value-add investment and decided to pursue a commercial wholesale.

As I honed my hunting skills, I began to realize that sometimes the best deals are not found through traditional channels. I started attending local real estate investor meetings and networking with other investors. This opened my eyes to the world of off-market deals and motivated sellers. One day, at a meeting, I met a fellow investor who was in financial distress and needed to sell one of his properties quickly. I was able to negotiate a favorable deal for both of us, and I added another property to my growing portfolio.

The art of the hunt is a skill that takes time and experience to develop. By cultivating patience, persistence, and a keen eye for detail, you can become a master hunter in the world of real estate. Remember that the best deals are often found where others are not looking. Network with other investors, attend local meetings, and always be on the lookout for opportunities. The perfect property is out there, waiting for you to discover it.

As you continue on your real estate investing journey, don't forget the lessons learned from José and the various stories shared in this chapter. Embrace the art of the hunt and remember that the real prize is not just the perfect property, but the growth, knowledge, and financial freedom that come with each successful investment. Keep pushing forward, stay curious, and never stop hunting for your next great opportunity.

Chapter 5

Financing Your Real Estate Investments

As I progressed in my real estate investing journey, I began to realize that finding the perfect property was only half the battle. The other half was figuring out how to finance the investment. After all, without the necessary funds, even the best deals would remain out of reach. I quickly discovered that financing your real estate investments is one of the secrets they don't want you to know. In this chapter, I will reveal various financing strategies and share my personal experiences, including the story of how I met Eduardo, a hard money lender who changed the way I approached financing.

One of the first financing methods I explored was seller financing. This is when the property owner agrees to finance the purchase of their property, essentially acting as the bank. This can be a win-win situation for both the buyer and the seller. The buyer gains access to financing without having to go through a traditional lender, while the seller may be able to sell their property more quickly and potentially receive a higher interest rate than they would by investing the proceeds elsewhere.

I'll never forget my first experience with seller financing. I had found a small duplex that was owned by a retired couple who were looking to sell and downsize. They were having trouble selling the property due to its outdated condition, and the local banks were hesitant to lend on it. Sensing an opportunity, I approached the couple with a seller financing proposal. To my delight, they agreed, and I was able to purchase the property with a low down payment and a reasonable interest rate. After making some renovations, I was able to increase the rents and create a positive cash flow.

Owner financing is another creative financing method. It is similar to seller financing but typically involves the owner holding a second mortgage on the property, allowing the buyer to obtain a traditional first mortgage from a bank. This can provide the buyer with additional leverage and reduce the amount of cash needed for a down payment.

I first encountered owner financing when purchasing a small triplex. The owner was eager to sell but understood that the property's condition might make it difficult for a buyer to secure a traditional bank loan. He agreed to hold a second mortgage on the property, which enabled me to obtain a loan from a local bank for the remainder of the purchase price. This allowed me to acquire the property with minimal cash out of pocket, and after making some improvements, I was able to refinance the property and pay off the owner's second mortgage.

As my real estate portfolio grew, I started to explore alternative financing options, which led me to meet Eduardo, a hard money lender. Hard money lenders are private individuals or companies that lend money based on the value of the property rather than the borrower's creditworthiness. They typically charge higher interest rates and fees than traditional banks but can often provide funding more quickly and with less stringent underwriting criteria.

Eduardo and I met at a local real estate investing seminar. We struck up a conversation, and he told me about his hard money lending business. Intrigued, I decided to give it a try when I found a fix-and-flip opportunity that required a quick closing. Thanks to Eduardo's fast and flexible financing, I was able to secure the property, complete the necessary renovations, and sell it for a profit. This experience opened my eyes to the power of hard money lending and the importance of having multiple financing options at my disposal.

Financing your real estate investments is a critical aspect of building a successful portfolio. By understanding and utilizing various financing methods, such as seller financing, owner financing, and hard money lending, you can unlock opportunities that may have otherwise been unattainable. The stories and experiences shared in this chapter serve as a reminder of the importance of being creative, resourceful, and open-minded when it comes to financing your real estate investments. Remember, the more financing options you have, the more flexibility you'll have in pursuing the perfect property.

As you continue your journey in real estate investing, keep an open mind and be willing to explore various financing strategies. Network with other investors, attend local meetings, and build relationships with lenders, both traditional and non-traditional. Knowledge is power, and understanding the different ways to finance your investments is a secret they don't want you to know.

By mastering the art of financing, you'll be better equipped to seize opportunities and build a successful real estate portfolio that generates wealth and financial freedom. Stay focused, persistent, and never stop learning.

Chapter 6

Building a Winning Team

As I continued to grow and expand my real estate investment portfolio, I quickly realized that I couldn't do it all alone. Success in real estate investing requires more than just knowledge and hard work; it requires a team of like-minded individuals who share the same vision and goals. Building a winning team is a real estate secret they don't want you to know. In this chapter, I will share my personal experiences in assembling my power team.

The importance of having a power team cannot be overstated. This group of professionals consists of money lenders, realtors, title companies, wholesalers, contractors, and more. Each member plays a critical role in the success of your real estate investments. They provide the expertise, support, and resources necessary to maximize your profits and minimize your risks.

I first realized the value of a power team when I attended a local real, estate investing seminar. The speaker emphasized the importance of surrounding yourself with individuals who complement their strengths and help overcome the, necessary tasks of buying, renovating, and managing properties. This concept resonated with me, and I immediately began searching for team members who could help me reach my real estate investing goals.

One of the best ways to find potential team members is to attend real estate meetups and seminars. These events provide an excellent opportunity to network with other investors and professionals in the industry. It was at one of these events that I met Kyle, a fellow real estate investor who would become a valuable member of my team.

Kyle and I hit it off right away. We shared a similar vision for our real estate investing careers and recognized that we could help each other grow and succeed. Kyle had a background in construction and was an expert in estimating repair costs and managing renovation projects. His skills complemented my own, and we quickly formed a partnership that allowed us to leverage our individual strengths for the benefit of our investments.

As our partnership flourished, we continued to build our power team. We found a reliable and knowledgeable realtor who understood the local market and could help us find undervalued properties. We also connected with a reputable title company that ensured smooth and efficient closings. Additionally, we developed relationships with wholesalers who could bring us off-market deals, providing us with an advantage over other investors.

One of our most critical team members was our contractor. A good contractor is worth their weight in gold, as they can make or break a renovation project. After interviewing several candidates, we finally found a contractor who shared our vision and commitment to quality work. With our team in place, we were able to tackle larger projects and scale our real estate investing business.

Building a winning team is a crucial component of success in real estate investing. By surrounding yourself with individuals who share your vision and possess the skills and expertise necessary to bring that vision to life, you can achieve greater success than you ever imagined. The story of my partnership with Kyle and the formation of our power team serves as a testament to the importance of collaboration and teamwork in the world of real estate investing.

As you continue on your journey, remember to focus on building relationships and nurturing your power team. Attend local events, network with other investors, and always be on the lookout for potential team members who can help you achieve your goals. With a winning team by your side, there's no limit to what you can accomplish in the world of real estate investing.

Building a winning team is a critical component of success in real estate investing.

Remember, together, you and your team can achieve far more than any one person could alone.

Chapter 7

The Art of Negotiation

As I delved deeper into the world of real estate investing, I came to understand that mastering the art of negotiation is an essential skill for success. Knowing how to negotiate effectively can make the difference between a mediocre deal and a highly profitable one. The art of negotiation in real estate is a secret they don't want you to know, and in this chapter, I'll share how this invaluable skill has benefited me, as well as the story of how I met my first mentor, in San Antonio.

In the early stages of my real estate investing journey, I quickly realized that negotiations were a critical aspect of every transaction. Whether I was negotiating the purchase price, repair costs, or rental terms, my ability to reach a mutually beneficial agreement directly impacted my bottom line. It was then that I decided to commit myself to mastering the art of negotiation.

I had been actively seeking a mentor to help me grow as an investor, and fate seemed to intervene when I attended a real estate conference in San Antonio. It was here that I met Armando, a seasoned real estate investor who would become my first mentor. Armando was giving a presentation on negotiation strategies at the conference, and I was captivated by his knowledge and experience. After the event, I approached him to express my gratitude for his insights. To my surprise, Armando offered to mentor me and help me hone my negotiation skills.

Armando taught me several invaluable lessons about negotiation. He emphasized the importance of doing thorough research and understanding the market, as well as the specific property and seller circumstances. This information would serve as the foundation for my negotiations, allowing me to present well-reasoned arguments and counteroffers. Armando also stressed the need to be flexible and adaptable, as each negotiation is unique and may require different approaches and tactics.

Over time, Armando and I developed a strong mentor-mentee relationship, and he continued to share his wisdom and insights with me. He showed me how to build rapport with sellers and other parties involved in the transaction, stressing the importance of establishing trust and credibility. Armando also taught me the value of knowing when to walk away from a deal, recognizing that not every negotiation would lead to a favorable outcome.

As I implemented Armando's teachings, I began to see significant improvements in my negotiation outcomes. I found that I was able to secure better deals, reduce my expenses, and increase my profits. The art of negotiation had become a powerful tool in my real estate investing toolbox.

Mastering the art of negotiation is a crucial skill for any real estate investor. By understanding the needs and motivations of the other party, conducting thorough research, and employing effective tactics like anchoring, you can greatly improve your ability to negotiate favorable deals. The story of my mentorship under Armando in San Antonio serves as a testament to the transformative power of honing your negotiation skills.

As you continue your journey in real estate investing, remember to invest time and effort into developing your negotiation abilities. Seek guidance from experienced investors like Armando, attend workshops, and practice your skills at every opportunity. With persistence and dedication, you can master the art of negotiation and unlock a world of possibilities in your real estate investing career.

Remember, successful negotiations are not about winning or losing; they're about finding solutions that benefit both parties and create lasting, profitable relationships in the world of real estate investing. With these valuable negotiation skills under your belt, you'll be well on your way to securing great deals and growing your investment portfolio. Remember, every successful negotiation brings you one step closer to achieving your real estate investing goals and dreams.

Chapter 8

Property Management

One day, as I was finishing up an intense workout at the gym, I overheard a conversation between two distressed-looking landlords. They were venting their frustrations about the challenges they faced in managing their rental properties, from chasing down rent payments to dealing with constant maintenance issues. Their conversation was a stark reminder of the importance of effective property management in the world of real estate investing.

Fortunately, early in my real estate investing journey, I had the opportunity to learn the secrets of successful property management from my friend and fellow investor, Adonai. Adonai had built an impressive portfolio of rental properties and had a system in place to ensure smooth operations. He shared with me that one of the real estate secrets they don't want you to know is that effective property management is the key to not having to worry about collecting rent from tenants or dealing with continuous issues.

Adonai had developed several strategies to manage his properties efficiently. One of the most significant factors in his success was his focus on building a solid team. He had a dedicated property manager overseeing each of his properties, responsible for addressing maintenance requests, handling tenant communications, and managing rent collection. By delegating these tasks to experienced professionals, Adonai could focus on expanding his portfolio and finding new investment opportunities.

Another important aspect of Adonai's property management strategy was preventative maintenance. He made sure that his property managers conducted regular inspections to identify potential issues before they escalated into costly repairs. By investing in routine maintenance, Adonai was able to keep his properties in excellent condition, attract and retain high-quality tenants, and avoid expensive emergencies.

Adonai also emphasized the importance of excellent communication with his tenants. He made it a priority to keep an open line of communication with his tenants, promptly addressing any concerns they raised and providing regular updates on maintenance or other property-related issues. By fostering positive relationships with his tenants, Adonai was able to minimize conflicts and keep tenant turnover low.

One of the most valuable lessons Adonai taught me was the importance of staying organized and keeping detailed records. Maintaining documentation of all rental payments, expenses, and maintenance requests can save you a lot of headaches and protect you in case of disputes or legal issues. Adonai used a property management software that helped him keep track of all his properties and stay organized.

Furthermore, Adonai stressed the importance of understanding local landlord-tenant laws and regulations. Being well-versed in these rules enabled him to navigate any legal issues that arose and protect his interests as a property owner. By staying informed and compliant with local regulations, Adonai minimized his exposure to potential lawsuits and costly fines.

The property management secrets I learned from Adonai had a profound impact on my real estate investing journey. By implementing his strategies, I was able to manage my properties effectively, avoid the headaches faced by the landlords at the gym, and ultimately build a more profitable and sustainable rental portfolio.

Effective property management is a critical aspect of real estate investing success. By developing systems and processes, screening tenants thoroughly, building relationships with reliable contractors, communicating with your tenants, and staying informed about laws and regulations, you'll unlock the basic real estate secrets that "they" don't want you to know. With the right approach to property management, you'll be well on your way to building a thriving and profitable real estate investment business.

Chapter 9

Buy and Hold Investing

During a casual conversation with a successful friend in the real estate business, I was introduced to the concept of buy and hold investing. As a young and ambitious investor, I was eager to learn and understand the strategies that could help me grow my wealth.

In this chapter, I will share with you the steps I've learned about buy and hold investing, as well as the secrets that "they" don't want you to know.

Step one: Focus on Cash Flow. One of the primary goals of buy and hold investing is to generate positive cash flow from your properties. This means ensuring that the rental income you collect is greater than the expenses associated with owning and managing the property.

In my early days as a real estate investor, I made sure to focus on properties with strong cash flow potential. By doing so, I was able to create a steady and reliable stream of income that would help me build wealth over time.

Step two: The Power of Leverage. Buy and hold investing also allows you to take advantage of leverage. By using other people's money (in the form of bank loans or private financing) to purchase properties, you can control a more significant portion of the market with less of your own capital.

When I began my buy and hold journey, I quickly realized the power of leverage in amplifying my investment returns. By utilizing loans and carefully managing my debt, I was able to grow my real estate portfolio rapidly.

Step three: Appreciation and Equity Growth. In addition to cash flow and leverage, buy and hold investing allows you to benefit from property appreciation and equity growth. As property values increase over time, so does the equity in your investment properties.

By focusing on well-located properties with strong growth potential, I was able to benefit from appreciation and equity growth, further increasing my net worth and providing additional opportunities for future investments.

Step four: Tax Advantages. Real estate investing, particularly buy and hold strategies, offers numerous tax advantages. These can include deductions for mortgage interest, property taxes, and depreciation, as well as the ability to defer capital gains taxes through a 1031 exchange.

As I became more experienced in buy and hold investing, I educated myself on the various tax benefits available and worked with a knowledgeable accountant to maximize my tax savings.

Step five: Patience and Long-term Thinking. Finally, one of the most important lessons I've learned in buy and hold investing is the value of patience and long-term thinking. Real estate investing is not a get-rich-quick scheme; it requires time, dedication, and a commitment to building wealth over the long term.

As I continued to grow my real estate portfolio, I focused on making smart, well-researched decisions and holding onto my properties for the long haul, allowing me to benefit from compounding returns and the wealth-building power of real estate.

Buy and hold investing is a powerful strategy for building wealth through real estate. By focusing on cash flow, leveraging other people's money, benefiting from appreciation and equity growth, maximizing tax advantages, and adopting a long-term mindset, you'll unlock the basic real estate secrets that "they" don't want you to know.

With persistence and dedication to these principles, you can build a successful and sustainable real estate investment business.

Chapter 10

Flipping Properties

When I first started my journey as a real estate investor, I had limited resources and needed a strategy that required little to no money to get started. Flipping houses was the answer. Flipping properties is a tactic where an investor buys a property, usually in need of repair, makes improvements, and then sells it for a profit. This method allowed me to build capital quickly, which then enabled me to reinvest in other real estate investments.

My first flip was a small, rundown house in the north side of San Antonio. I knew that with some work, this house could become a beautiful home for a family. I also knew that the neighborhood was in demand, which meant there was potential for profit. This was a perfect opportunity for me to apply the flipping techniques I'd learned and create something valuable.

Before jumping into the project, I had to ensure that I fully understood the numbers involved in the deal. This meant analyzing comparables (comps) and calculating the After Repair Value (ARV). Comps are recently sold properties in the area that are similar to the subject property, and they help establish a realistic selling price for the flip. ARV is an estimate of what the property will be worth once the renovations are completed, and it's crucial for determining your potential profit.

To be successful in flipping properties, it's essential to master several key techniques:

Know your market: Understanding the local real estate market is critical to your success as a flipper. Research the neighborhoods, the demographics, and the housing trends. This will help you determine which properties have the most potential for profit.

Analyze comps and calculate ARV: Use comps to determine a realistic selling price for your flip. Calculate the ARV by estimating the cost of repairs and improvements and adding it to the property's purchase price. Make sure the numbers work in your favor before committing to a flip.

Build a reliable construction team: Having a trustworthy team of contractors and subcontractors is crucial to completing renovations on time and within budget. Take the time to find and vet professionals who can deliver quality work and have a proven track record.

Cultivate relationships with realtors and title companies: Having a solid network of professionals in your corner can make all the difference in your flipping business. They can help you find deals, navigate the buying and selling process, and ensure that everything goes smoothly.

Master the art of finding deals: Learn how to spot undervalued properties with potential for profit. This can involve researching foreclosures, attending auctions, or using online resources to find properties in need of repair.

Budget wisely and stick to your numbers: Before starting any renovation project, create a detailed budget and stick to it. This will help you avoid overspending and ensure that you make a profit on your investment.

Time is money: The longer a property sits on the market, the more it costs you in holding costs. Make sure your renovations are completed quickly and efficiently, and price the property correctly to sell quickly.

With these techniques in mind, I tackled my first flip in San Antonio. I assembled a team of professionals, including a general contractor, a project manager, and various subcontractors. Together, we devised a plan to transform the house into a beautiful, modern home.

Once the renovations were complete, it was time to put the house on the market. The key to a successful flip is to price it correctly. Overpricing the property can lead to it sitting on the market for too long, while underpricing it can result in a smaller profit margin. With the help of a real estate agent, I priced the house just right, and it sold quickly for a nice profit.

Flipping properties was an invaluable strategy for me in the beginning of my real estate journey. It allowed me to generate quick profits, learn the ins and outs of the real estate market, and create a strong network of professionals. Flipping houses taught me valuable lessons about project management, budgeting, and negotiation, which I have carried with me throughout my career.

As I continued to flip properties, I honed my skills and developed an eye for identifying properties with great potential.

Flipping properties is one of the real estate secrets that "they" don't want you to know. It's a strategy that, when executed correctly, can lead to substantial profits and set the foundation for a successful real estate investment career. As you embark on your own flipping journey, remember the techniques I've shared and never underestimate the power of determination and hard work. With the right mindset, knowledge, and network, you too can transform properties and create a thriving real estate empire.

Chapter 11

The Wealthy Investor's Mentality

I still remember that hot summer afternoon in our small Texas town when my friend Robert and I, just kids at the time, sat under the shade of a large oak tree in my backyard. We were in our early teens and had just started to dream big. With our heads full of aspirations, we had the whole world ahead of us.

As we munched on salty popcorn and sipped ice-cold sodas, we talked about our futures and what we wanted to achieve in life. We both dreamed of becoming successful entrepreneurs, and even at that young age, we were drawn to the idea of investing in real estate. Little did we know that the wealthy investor's mentality we would later develop would be one of the real estate secrets they don't want you to know.

Instead of following the conventional path of attending college, Robert and I decided to dive headfirst into the world of real estate. We believed that our passion and determination would be enough to drive our success. We were eager to learn from our experiences, and we knew that cultivating a wealthy investor's mentality would be the key to unlocking our full potential.

Our early years in real estate were filled with challenges and valuable lessons. We spent countless hours studying the market, attending seminars, and seeking mentorship from experienced investors. As our knowledge and experience grew, we began to understand the importance of adopting a wealthy investor's mentality.

One day, as we sat in a coffee shop reminiscing about our journey, we recalled that childhood memory under the oak tree. We realized that even back then, we had the seeds of a wealthy investor's mentality within us. We were always curious, eager to learn, and had an unyielding determination to succeed.

Over the years, we nurtured those seeds, and our mindset began to take shape. We understood that having a wealthy investor's mentality meant more than just knowing the ins and outs of the real estate market. It meant developing a resilient mindset, being able to adapt to change, and having the courage to take calculated risks.

As our careers progressed, we discovered that the wealthy investor's mentality was indeed one of the real estate secrets they don't want you to know. Those who possess this mentality are better equipped to spot opportunities, make smarter investment decisions, and ultimately achieve greater success.

Today, Robert and I are successful real estate investors, but we never forget the lessons from our past. We continue to cultivate our wealthy investor's mentality by staying curious, learning from our experiences, and surrounding ourselves with like-minded individuals who share our passion for success.

We also understand the importance of giving back and passing on the knowledge we've gained throughout our journey. We mentor aspiring investors and share our insights, hoping to inspire others to develop their own wealthy investor's mentality and unlock the secrets to success in real estate.

That hot summer day under the oak tree may be a distant memory, but the seeds of our wealthy investor's mentality continue to grow and flourish. It's a mindset that has served us well on our journey to success, and one that we're committed to nurturing for the rest of our lives. By sharing our story, we hope to encourage others to embrace the real estate secrets they don't want you to know, chase their dreams, and achieve the success they desire. And as we continue on this path, we're reminded of the importance of lifelong learning and personal growth, reinforcing the notion that the wealthy investor's mentality is truly one of the most powerful tools in the world of real estate.

But perhaps the most important thing is to never stop learning and growing. Real estate investing is a constantly evolving field, and the most successful investors are those who are willing to adapt and change with the times.

Remember to adopt the wealthy investor's mentality. Be willing to take risks, be patient, think outside the box, and focus on creating value. With the right mindset, anything is possible in the world of real estate investing.

Chapter 12

Learning the Language

It was an early Saturday when I found myself sitting in the back row of a real estate seminar, eagerly taking notes as the speaker passionately shared his knowledge on the industry. At that moment, I realized that to succeed in real estate, I needed to become fluent in the language of the industry. Just like learning any new language, this required dedication, practice, and perseverance.

Growing up in a Hispanic household, learning a new language was not unfamiliar territory for me. My family spoke Spanish at home, and from a young age, I had to learn English in school. I remember the countless hours spent practicing, the challenges I faced, and the feeling of accomplishment when I could finally communicate with ease. This early experience with language learning would later become an invaluable lesson as I delved into the world of real estate.

As I began my journey into real estate investing, I quickly realized that learning the language was a secret they don't want you to know about. The industry was filled with jargon, acronyms, and complex terms that were difficult to understand without a solid foundation. This was not by accident; it was a barrier of entry, a way to keep newcomers at bay.

I was determined not to let this hurdle deter me from my path to success. I set out on a quest to learn the language of real estate, just as I had learned English years before. I started with the basics, familiarizing myself with terms such as "amortization," "cap rate," "cash flow," and "equity." I studied tirelessly, devouring every book, article, and podcast I could find on the subject.

It was during this period that I met my first mentor, a seasoned San Antonio real estate investor who took me under his wing. He saw my dedication to learning the language and recognized my potential for success in the industry. With his guidance, I began to immerse myself in the world of real estate, attending meetings, networking events, and seminars.

In those settings, I was surrounded by industry professionals, listening to their conversations, and picking up on the nuances of their language. I started to recognize the importance of understanding the language, not only to comprehend complex concepts but also to engage with others in the field.

As I continued to learn the language, I started to see patterns and connections that were previously hidden from me. The once daunting terms began to make sense, and I could see how they fit together like pieces of a puzzle. I was gaining the confidence to engage in conversations, ask questions, and even contribute my own thoughts and ideas.

Over time, I became fluent in the language of real estate, a fluency that proved to be crucial to my success as an investor. It allowed me to understand the intricacies of deals, analyze properties, and negotiate with confidence. I was no longer an outsider looking in; I was an active participant in the world of real estate.

Learning the language of real estate was one of the most significant steps I took toward achieving my goals in the industry. It opened doors to opportunities and connections that would have been impossible to access otherwise. I discovered that knowledge is power, and the ability to speak the language of real estate gave me the power to succeed.

As I reflect on my journey, I can't help but think of my childhood experiences learning English. Just like mastering a new language, learning the language of real estate required dedication, practice, and perseverance. And just like with any language, fluency came with time, experience, and exposure.

I encourage you, as you embark on your own real estate journey, to learn the language of the industry. Embrace the challenge, dedicate yourself to the process, and find a mentor or community to support you along the way. The secret to success in real estate lies in your ability to understand and communicate effectively in its unique language. Once you have mastered this skill, the world of real estate will open up to you, providing endless opportunities for growth, connections, and success.

Never underestimate the power of learning the language of real estate. It may seem daunting at first, but with dedication, practice, and perseverance, you can become fluent and unlock the secrets they don't want you to know. In doing so, you will be well-equipped to navigate the complex world of real estate and, ultimately, achieve your goals as an investor.

Remember, the journey of a thousand miles begins with a single step. Start by immersing yourself in the language, and soon, you will find that you have become a part of the real estate community. As you continue to grow and evolve as an investor, never stop learning and improving your understanding of the industry's language. The more fluent you become, the more successful you will be.

Embrace the challenge, and you will soon find yourself among the ranks of the most successful real estate investors.

Chapter 13

The Importance of Financial Education

From a young age, I had a burning desire to succeed and a thirst for knowledge. I knew that I wanted to make a difference in the world and build a life of financial freedom for myself and my family. But I quickly realized that to truly excel in the world of real estate, I needed more than just passion and determination. I needed a solid foundation in financial education.

Growing up, discussions about money were sparse in my household. Like many others, I picked up bits and pieces of financial wisdom from my mother and through trial and error. Realizing the importance of a comprehensive financial education, I embarked on a journey to learn everything I could about money management, investment strategies, and wealth-building techniques. I devoured books, attended seminars, and sought mentorship from successful real estate investors. And as my knowledge grew, so did my confidence and success in the industry.

One day, I met a young man named Alex at a real estate seminar. He approached me during a break, and we struck up a conversation. Like me, Alex had a hunger for success and was eager to learn the ins and outs of real estate investing. As we chatted, I could see the potential in him, but I also recognized that he, too, lacked a solid financial education.

Over the next few months, I took Alex under my wing and helped coach him in his real estate investment journey. We discussed the importance of understanding assets and liabilities, the power of leveraging other people's money, and the significance of cash flow management. I shared with him the real estate secrets they don't want you to know, including the crucial role financial education plays in achieving lasting success.

As Alex's understanding of financial concepts grew, so did his proficiency in real estate investing. He began to make smarter investment decisions, effectively managing his properties and steadily growing his portfolio. In particular, Alex became highly skilled at identifying and flipping homes in San Antonio. He developed a keen eye for spotting undervalued properties, negotiating the best deals, and making the necessary improvements to maximize his profits. Within a short span of time, he had successfully flipped numerous homes and earned a reputation as a savvy investor in the local real estate community.

Watching his progress, I couldn't help but feel a sense of pride in knowing that I had played a part in his development as an investor. Throughout our time together, Alex and I often reflected on the importance of financial education. It was clear to both of us that this crucial knowledge was one of the real estate secrets they don't want you to know. By equipping ourselves with a strong foundation in financial literacy, we were better prepared to navigate the often-turbulent waters of the real estate world and make sound investment decisions that would ultimately lead to our success.

Today, as I continue to work with aspiring investors, I am more convinced than ever of the importance of financial education. It is my belief that a well-rounded understanding of money management, investment strategies, and wealth-building techniques is the key to unlocking one's full potential in the world of real estate. By sharing my own experiences and the lessons I've learned along the way, I hope to inspire others to seek out the knowledge that will empower them to take control of their financial futures and achieve the success they so richly deserve.

I encourage you to embark on your own journey of financial education, whether you're just starting in the world of real estate investing or are a seasoned professional. The knowledge you gain will not only help you navigate the industry with confidence, but it will also enable you to build a legacy of wealth for yourself and future generations. Remember, the real estate secrets they don't want you to know are within your grasp all it takes is a commitment to learning and the willingness to grow.

As you continue on your path to financial freedom and success in real estate, remember to stay true to your values and maintain the wealthy investor's mentality. Surround yourself with like-minded individuals who share your passion for knowledge and growth. Learn from those who have come before you and are willing to share their wisdom and experiences. Always be open to new ideas and strategies, but be discerning in what you choose to implement in your own investment portfolio.

Most importantly, never forget the importance of giving back. As you climb the ladder of success, remember to reach down and help others on their journey as well. Share your knowledge, your time, and your resources with those who are eager to learn and grow. This, too, is part of the wealthy investor's mentality and one of the secrets they don't want you to know.

Remember, In the world of real estate investing, there will always be challenges and obstacles to overcome.

Chapter 14

Passive Income and Financial Freedom

Throughout my real estate investing journey, one overarching goal has remained at the forefront of my endeavors: achieving passive income and financial freedom. These two objectives are integral to making it as a real estate investor and provide the foundation for lasting success. In this chapter, I'll share how my friend and mentor Tom taught me the principles of passive income and financial freedom, and how they've shaped my investing strategies.

I met Tom at a real estate seminar a few years into my investing career. He was a seasoned investor who had built an impressive portfolio of income generating properties. Over time, Tom became both a friend and a mentor, sharing his knowledge and experiences with me. Our conversations often revolved around various investment strategies, market trends, and the importance of persistence in the face of challenges. One of the most valuable lessons Tom taught me was the importance of focusing on passive income and financial freedom.

Tom explained that passive income is money earned with little to no effort on the part of the investor. In the context of real estate, this means acquiring rental properties that generate consistent cash flow with minimal involvement. Financial freedom, on the other hand, is achieved when passive income surpasses living expenses, allowing the investor to live life on their own terms without being dependent on a traditional job.

Armed with this knowledge, I shifted my focus towards acquiring properties that would generate passive income and ultimately lead to financial freedom. Tom shared several strategies for identifying and acquiring these types of properties, including searching for undervalued assets in up and coming neighborhoods, focusing on multi unit properties, and leveraging creative financing options. He also emphasized the importance of networking and building relationships with other investors, real estate agents, and property managers, as these connections could lead to valuable insights and opportunities.

One memorable deal that Tom and I worked on together was a partnership on a house flip in a desirable neighborhood. Tom had identified the property as a promising investment opportunity due to its potential for significant profit after renovations. We joined forces on the project, with Tom contributing his expertise in property analysis and me managing the renovation process. After completing the renovations and putting the property on the market, we were able to sell it quickly for a substantial profit. This experience not only bolstered my confidence as an investor but also reinforced the importance of collaboration and the power of various income streams in achieving financial freedom.

One of the key principles Tom emphasized was the importance of diligently managing properties to maximize cash flow. This included ensuring properties were well-maintained, vacancies were minimized, and rents were set at appropriate levels. By applying these principles, I was able to steadily increase my passive income and edge closer to financial freedom.

Tom also taught me the value of diversifying my investment portfolio. Rather than focusing solely on residential properties, he encouraged me to explore other types of real estate investments, such as commercial properties and real estate investment trusts (REITs). By diversifying my portfolio, I was able to mitigate risk and create multiple streams of passive income.

Passive income and financial freedom are central to the success of any real estate investor. By focusing on acquiring income-generating properties, diligently managing them, and diversifying your portfolio, you can steadily build wealth and work towards financial independence. The lessons I learned from my friend and mentor Tom have been instrumental in shaping my investing strategies and guiding me on the path to financial freedom.

As you continue your real estate investing journey, always keep the principles of passive income and financial freedom in mind. By doing so, you'll be well on your way to achieving the success and financial independence you desire.

Chapter 15

Understanding Assets and Liabilities

It was the best of times for my friend Alfonso. He had just landed his dream job with a six-figure salary and decided to reward himself by purchasing a brand new luxurious 5,000 sqft home in a country club community in San Antonio. He threw an extravagant housewarming party, inviting everyone he knew, including me, to celebrate his success. The house was spectacular, and I couldn't help but feel a twinge of envy as I admired the stunning architecture, beautifully landscaped backyard, and the designer interiors.

Two years later, the worst of times arrived. The company Alfonso worked for went bankrupt, and he lost his job. Unable to keep up with his mortgage payments, he was forced to sell his home at a significant loss. As we sat together at a local fast food restaurant, eating burgers and fries, I listened intently to his story. I couldn't help but think about the importance of understanding assets and liabilities. That knowledge could have prevented Alfonso from falling into a financial crisis.

Alfonso confided in me that he had never really understood the difference between assets and liabilities before buying the house. He had been seduced by the glamour of living in a prestigious neighborhood and had assumed that owning such a property would only increase his wealth. He never anticipated that his home could become a financial burden.

As a real estate investor, I've come to realize that understanding assets and liabilities is a secret that most people are never taught. It's a fundamental concept that can make all the difference between financial success and failure, especially in real estate investing.

An asset is something that puts money in your pocket. In real estate, this could be rental income from an apartment building, a commercial property, or even a single family home. On the other hand, a liability is something that takes money out of your pocket. For most people, their primary residence is a liability, as it requires mortgage payments, property taxes, and maintenance expenses.

The key to building wealth in real estate is to focus on acquiring assets while minimizing liabilities. By doing so, you'll create a steady stream of passive income that can cover your living expenses and fund the lifestyle you desire. Instead of using your hard earned money to pay for toys, cars, boats, and country club memberships, your assets will cover those costs, leaving you free to enjoy life without financial stress.

But why is this knowledge considered a secret? The truth is, many financial institutions and industries don't want you to know about the power of assets because it would disrupt their business model. They profit from people taking on debt to buy liabilities such as expensive homes, cars, and other consumer goods. By keeping the masses in the dark about the true nature of assets and liabilities, they maintain control over their finances.

As a real estate investor, my journey to understanding assets and liabilities began by learning to differentiate between the two. I started by analyzing my own financial situation, listing all my assets and liabilities on a piece of paper. This exercise allowed me to clearly see where my money was going and which investments were actually working for me.

Next, I set a goal to increase my assets and decrease my liabilities. I focused on investing in properties that generated positive cash flow, ensuring that my assets would continually grow and pay for my desired lifestyle. By doing so, I was able to achieve financial freedom and no longer had to rely on a traditional job to make ends meet.

I shared my experiences with Alfonso, hoping that my story would inspire him to learn more about assets and liabilities. He listened carefully and asked questions, showing a genuine interest in understanding the concepts I was explaining. I could see a glimmer of hope in his eyes, as he realized that it was not too late for him to change his financial situation.

Over the next few months, Alfonso and I spent countless hours discussing real estate investing, assets, and liabilities. He began reading books, attending seminars, and seeking out successful real estate investors as mentors. With renewed determination, Alfonso set out to rebuild his financial life. He started by downsizing to a more affordable home and focused on paying off his debts. Once he was debt free, he began researching investment properties that could generate passive income.

My friend Alfonso's story is a cautionary tale that highlights the importance of understanding assets and liabilities. By grasping this fundamental concept, you can build a solid foundation for wealth creation through real estate investing. Don't let the secret stay hidden; use this knowledge to your advantage and watch your financial dreams become a reality.

Remember, it's never too late to learn and change your financial destiny.

Chapter 16

Finding Your Niche

It was a warm spring evening when I met Ryan, a young and ambitious entrepreneur who was just starting on his real estate investing journey. We were both attending a real estate networking event in San Antonio, and Ryan eagerly approached me to discuss his newly found passion for the industry. As we exchanged stories, I couldn't help but notice the glint in Ryan's eyes, a familiar fire that I recognized from my early days in the business.

Before diving into our conversation, Ryan shared a bit of his background. He had been working in the corporate world for several years but had recently decided to leave the security of a 9 to 5 job to pursue his dream of becoming a real estate investor. Ryan was hungry for knowledge and eager to learn about every aspect of the real estate world, from flipping houses to managing rental properties, wholesaling, and even commercial real estate. While his enthusiasm was commendable, I couldn't help but think about one of the most important real estate secrets they don't want you to know: the power of finding your niche.

As we sat down for a cup of coffee, I shared my thoughts with Ryan. "While it's great to have a wide range of interests in real estate, it's crucial to focus on finding your niche," I said. "Being a jack of all trades can actually hold you back in this industry."

Ryan looked puzzled, so I continued, "By concentrating on one specific area of real estate, you can become an expert in that niche, which will ultimately lead to greater success. It's one of the real estate secrets they don't want you to know, because they want to keep you distracted and spread thin."

I shared my own experience of finding my niche in the real estate world. In the beginning, I dabbled in various aspects of the industry, but it wasn't until I focused on multi family properties that my career truly took off. By concentrating my efforts on one area, I was able to develop an in-depth understanding of the market, which allowed me to make smarter investments and achieve greater success.

As we continued our conversation, I could see that Ryan was starting to understand the importance of finding a niche. We discussed the various areas of real estate investing he could explore, and I encouraged him to attend workshops, network with other investors, and gain hands-on experience to help him identify his ideal niche.

Over the following months, Ryan and I kept in touch, and I was pleased to see him embrace the concept of finding his niche. He decided to focus on fix-and-flip properties in up-and-coming neighborhoods, a niche that suited his passion for design and renovation. With this newfound focus, Ryan's real estate career began to flourish, and he started to build a name for himself in the local market.

As I reflect on my encounter with Ryan, I am reminded of my mission with this book: to help entrepreneurs become better entrepreneurs by sharing the real estate secrets they don't want you to know. By revealing the importance of finding your niche, I hope to inspire others to hone in on their own areas of expertise and unlock their full potential in the world of real estate investing.

In this competitive industry, finding your niche is more than just a smart strategy; it's a powerful secret that can propel you toward greater success. By sharing my experiences and the lessons I've learned along the way, I aim to empower fellow entrepreneurs to find their own path in the world of real estate, armed with the knowledge of the secrets they don't want you to know. And as I continue to watch Ryan's progress, I'm proud to have played a small part in helping him forge his own successful path in this exciting industry.

Finding your niche in the world of real estate investing is a critical step on the path to success and financial freedom. By focusing on a specific area of the market that aligns with your interests and strengths, you can unlock the basic secrets they don't want you to know and build lasting wealth through strategic investments.

The key to success lies in your ability to focus, build your expertise, and adapt to the ever changing world of real estate investing.

Remember, by honing in on your unique strengths and interests, and by arming yourself with the knowledge of the secrets they don't want you to know, you'll be well on your way to achieving financial freedom and making a lasting impact in the exciting world of real estate investing.

Chapter 17

Investing in Multi Family Properties

A warm breeze blew through the open window, gently rustling the papers on my desk as I prepared for another day in the world of real estate investing. I remember feeling a sense of anticipation and excitement as I sipped my coffee and gazed out over the San Antonio skyline, reflecting on the journey that had led me to this point. The world of multi family property investing had been a game changer for me, providing the opportunity to unlock the basic real estate secrets they don't want you to know.

As I sat at my desk, I recalled the conversation that had sparked my interest in multi family properties. It was a sunny afternoon, and I was having lunch with a fellow investor named Juan, who had found great success in the world of multi family investing. As we shared stories and insights, he told me about the unique benefits of investing in properties with multiple units, such as duplexes, triplexes, and apartment buildings.

Juan painted a vivid picture of the potential for passive income and wealth-building that multi family properties offered. He spoke of the stability provided by multiple streams of rental income and the reduced risk associated with vacancies. As he described the economies of scale that could be achieved through efficient property management and maintenance, I could feel the gears in my mind turning, as I began to see the possibilities that lay ahead.

As I listened to Juan's stories and experiences, I realized that multi family investing was an opportunity I couldn't afford to ignore. I knew that if I could learn the ins and outs of this niche within the real estate market, I could unlock the basic secrets they don't want you to know and take my investing journey to new heights.

Emboldened by my conversation with Juan, I set out to acquire my first multi family property. I knew that finding the right property would be critical to my success, so I began my search by focusing on factors such as location, property condition, and potential for appreciation. I spent countless hours researching neighborhoods, attending open houses, and analyzing potential investments to find the perfect fit.

Finally, after months of searching, I found a charming duplex in a desirable neighborhood with strong rental demand. The property needed some minor repairs and updates, but I could see the potential for strong cash flow and long term appreciation. I moved forward with the purchase and began the process of financing, renovations, and finding tenants for the property.

As I dove deeper into the world of multi family investing, I quickly learned that effective property management was critical to my success. I experimented with managing the property myself, but soon discovered that working with a professional property management company was a wise investment. This allowed me to focus on growing my portfolio and seeking new opportunities while ensuring the day to day operations of my property were handled efficiently.

Over time, I continued to acquire additional multi family properties, honing my skills and learning valuable lessons along the way. I discovered the importance of building relationships with local lenders and exploring creative financing strategies to fund my investments. I also learned the value of networking with other real estate professionals, attending industry events, and staying up-to-date on the latest trends and opportunities within my niche.

As I gazed out my window that morning, I felt a sense of gratitude and excitement for the opportunities that lay ahead in my multi family investing journey. I knew that this path would not be without its challenges, but I also knew that the rewards and potential for financial freedom made it a journey worth pursuing. With each new property and experience, I continued to unlock the basic real estate secrets they don't want you to know, allowing me to build wealth and create a solid foundation for my financial future.

Investing in multi family properties can be a powerful and rewarding strategy for those looking to build wealth and achieve financial freedom through real estate investing. By understanding the unique benefits, challenges, and opportunities associated with multi family investments, you can set yourself on a path to success and unlock the secrets that others may not want you to discover.

As you pursue your own multi family investing journey, remember the lessons and insights shared in this chapter. Be diligent in your research, build strong relationships within the industry, and never stop learning and growing as an investor.

Chapter 18

The Art of Real Estate Wholesaling

I arrived at the bustling coffee shop just in time to catch a glimpse of my old friend and fellow investor, Adonai, settling into a cozy corner with a warm smile on his face. He had recently discovered a niche in the real estate world that was rapidly changing his life. Little did I know that our conversation that evening would introduce me to the world of real estate wholesaling, a strategy that held the potential to unlock the basic real estate secrets they don't want you to know.

As we settled into our seats with steaming cups of coffee, Adonai's eyes sparkled with enthusiasm as he began to explain his latest venture. Real estate wholesaling, he told me, was a strategy that allowed him to connect motivated sellers with eager buyers, all without ever taking ownership of the property. In return, he earned a profit for his efforts in bringing the deal together.

Adonai continued, explaining that this approach allowed him to generate income without the need for large capital investments or the risk associated with purchasing and holding property. As he described the process of finding deals, negotiating contracts, and connecting with buyers, I couldn't help but feel intrigued by this new world of opportunity that was unfolding before me.

Adonai was kind enough to share his insights and experiences as a real estate wholesaler, providing me with the building blocks I needed to get started. He explained that the first step in wholesaling was to find motivated sellers, often individuals facing financial difficulties or looking to unload a property quickly. By tapping into his network, advertising, and even driving around neighborhoods, he was able to identify potential leads and make contact with these sellers.

Once he had identified a promising lead, Adonai would then negotiate a purchase contract with the seller, locking in a price that allowed for a profit margin. It was crucial, he emphasized, to include a clause that allowed him to assign the contract to a buyer, ensuring that he was not obligated to follow through with the purchase himself.

With a contract in hand, Adonai would then turn his attention to finding an end buyer typically a real estate investor who was interested in purchasing the property. He would present the deal to potential buyers, highlighting the profit potential and other advantages of the property. If the buyer was interested, he would then assign the contract to them, allowing them to step into his shoes and complete the purchase directly from the seller.

Upon the closing of the deal, Adonai would receive his "wholesale fee" the difference between the price he had negotiated with the seller and the price the buyer was willing to pay. This fee, he explained, was his reward for connecting the parties and facilitating the transaction.

Inspired by Adonai's success and the potential for financial freedom that real estate wholesaling offered, I decided to immersed myself in the world of real estate wholesaling. Networking with other investors, attending seminars, and constantly seeking new opportunities to learn and grow.

As I honed my skills as a wholesaler, I discovered that the key to success in this niche was persistence, creativity, and an ability to build strong relationships within the industry. By staying focused on my goals and staying true to my values, I was able to unlock the basic real estate secrets they don't want you to know and create a profitable business built on the foundation of connecting opportunities.

As I look back on my journey into the world of real estate wholesaling, I am grateful for the lessons, experiences, and relationships that have shaped my success in this niche. Through wholesaling, I have been able to create a stream of income that has not only supported my financial goals but also allowed me to help others in the process. By connecting motivated sellers with eager buyers, I have played a part in transforming lives and communities for the better.

Real estate wholesaling is not without its challenges, but the rewards can be significant for those who are willing to put in the effort and dedication required to succeed. By understanding the process, building a network of industry professionals, and continually seeking out opportunities to learn and grow, wholesalers can unlock the basic real estate secrets they don't want you to know.

The road to success in wholesaling is paved with challenges, but by embracing these hurdles and treating them as opportunities for growth, wholesalers can unlock the basic real estate secrets they don't want you to know.

The rewards of real estate wholesaling extend far beyond the financial gains. The experiences, relationships, and personal growth that accompany this journey have the potential to shape you into a more resilient, resourceful, and compassionate individual, capable of making a lasting impact in the world of real estate and beyond.

Chapter 19

Location, Location, Location

One sunny and humid afternoon, I found myself walking through a quaint neighborhood in San Antonio Texas, admiring the beautifully landscaped yards and charming houses. It was here that I came across a scene that would forever change the way I approached real estate investing: a young couple standing outside a newly purchased home, beaming with pride and joy as they posed for a photograph with their real estate agent.

As I continued on my way, I couldn't help but wonder what it was about this particular neighborhood that made it so special. What made this location so desirable that it could bring such happiness to a young family and undoubtedly provide a solid investment for their future? The answer, I would soon come to realize, was the power of location, location, location.

As I delved deeper into the world of real estate investing, I became increasingly aware of the importance of location when it came to selecting and evaluating properties. It wasn't enough to find a beautiful house or a well-maintained building; the true value of a property was intrinsically tied to its location and the potential for growth and development in the surrounding area.

I learned that properties in good locations would not only attract higher quality tenants but would also appreciate in value more quickly and reliably than those in less desirable areas. With this knowledge in hand, I set out to uncover the secrets of identifying prime locations that would maximize my investment returns and provide a strong foundation for my real estate portfolio.

What Makes a Location Desirable? As I began to study various markets and neighborhoods, I discovered that there were several key factors that contributed to the desirability of a location. These factors, when present, could create a powerful synergy that would drive demand, increase property values, and ultimately lead to a thriving and successful real estate investment.

Some of the key factors I learned to look for included:

Accessibility: Properties that were easily accessible by major roads, highways, and public transportation tended to be more desirable to both buyers and renters.

Economic Growth: Areas with a strong local economy, job opportunities, and a growing population were more likely to experience increased demand for housing, leading to higher property values and rental rates.

Amenities: Neighborhoods with desirable amenities, such as quality schools, parks, shopping centers, and recreational facilities, would attract higher quality tenants and command higher rents.

Safety and Security: Properties in safe, well-maintained neighborhoods were more attractive to potential buyers and renters, who were willing to pay a premium for the peace of mind that came with living in a secure community.

With these key factors in mind, I set out to refine my skills in identifying prime real estate locations. I spent countless hours researching neighborhoods, analyzing market trends, and speaking with local experts to gain insights into the factors that drove demand and growth in various areas.

Over time, I developed a keen eye for spotting the subtle indicators that signaled a neighborhood was on the verge of growth and transformation. By paying attention to planned infrastructure improvements, new commercial developments, and shifting demographics, I was able to identify locations that held the potential for significant appreciation in property values over time.

Location, Location, Location. As I built my real estate portfolio, I found that the power of location could not be underestimated. By focusing my efforts on properties in prime locations, I was able to generate higher rental incomes, attract quality tenants, and realize substantial gains in property values.

More than just a catchy phrase, "location, location, location" became the guiding principle of my real estate investing strategy. By understanding the factors that contribute to a desirable location and honing the skills to identify prime opportunities, I was able to unlock the basic real estate secrets that others didn't want me to know.

The importance of location in real estate investing cannot be overstated. By carefully considering factors such as accessibility, economic growth, amenities, and safety, investors can make informed decisions that maximize the potential for success and profitability in their real estate endeavors.

As you venture forth in your own real estate journey, remember the power of location, location, location. With this knowledge in hand, you will be well on your way to building a successful real estate portfolio and securing a prosperous future for yourself and those around you. Keep learning, growing, and seeking out new opportunities to create lasting value in the world of real estate.

Chapter 20

The Art of Due Diligence

I t was an early morning when I met with my mentor, Armando, at his commercial building in the Alamo city. As we discussed the latest trends in the real estate market, he asked me a question that would forever change the way I approached my investments: "Alberto, have you ever heard of due diligence?"

At that time, I was relatively new to the world of real estate investing, and the concept of due diligence was unfamiliar to me. As Armando began to explain the importance of conducting thorough research and analysis before making any investment decisions, I quickly realized that mastering the art of due diligence would be essential to my success as a real estate investor.

Understanding Due Diligence. Due diligence, as Armando explained, is the process of carefully investigating and evaluating a property or investment opportunity before committing any resources. It involves gathering and analyzing information about the property, its financial performance, the local market, and any potential risks or challenges that may affect its value or profitability.

The purpose of due diligence is to minimize risk and ensure that you are making informed decisions based on accurate and reliable information. As a real estate investor, conducting thorough due diligence is crucial to avoiding costly mistakes and maximizing the potential for success in your investments.

The Due Diligence Process. As I delved deeper into the world of real estate investing, I began to develop my own due diligence process, guided by the lessons and insights I had gained from Armando and other industry experts. My process involved several key steps, which I will outline below:

Property Analysis: First and foremost, I would conduct a thorough inspection of the property itself, assessing its condition, features, and any potential issues that may require repair or renovation. This would help me determine the true value of the property and the costs associated with bringing it up to its full potential.

Financial Analysis: Next, I would review the property's financial performance, including its rental income, expenses, and cash flow. By analyzing these figures, I could determine whether the property was a good investment and what kind of return I could expect.

Market Research: To gain a better understanding of the local market, I would research current trends, rental rates, and property values in the area. This would help me identify any potential risks or opportunities and make more informed decisions about my investments.

Legal and Regulatory Review: Lastly, I would consult with legal and regulatory experts to ensure that I was aware of any zoning restrictions, building codes, or other regulations that may affect my plans for the property.

The Power of Due Diligence. As I applied these due diligence principles to my real estate investments, I quickly realized the value of this meticulous approach. By conducting thorough research and analysis, I was able to uncover hidden opportunities and avoid potential pitfalls that could have derailed my investment plans.

Moreover, I discovered that the art of due diligence was not limited to the initial stages of the investment process. By continually monitoring my properties and staying informed about changes in the market, I was able to make timely and strategic decisions that enhanced the value and profitability of my real estate portfolio.

Uncovering the Basic Real Estate Secrets They Don't Want You to Know. As I reflect on my journey in the world of real estate investing, I am grateful for the lessons and insights that have shaped my success. The art of due diligence, in particular, has been instrumental in helping me uncover the basic real estate secrets they don't want you to know.

By embracing the power of due diligence, you too can unlock the hidden potential of your real estate investments and create a strong foundation for lasting success. As you venture forth on your own journey in real estate, remember the importance of conducting thorough research and analysis before making any investment decisions. With this knowledge in hand, you will be well-equipped to navigate the complexities of the market, minimize risk, and maximize the potential for success in your endeavors.

Mastering the art of due diligence is an essential skill for any aspiring real estate investor. By taking the time to carefully investigate and evaluate every aspect of a potential investment, you can make informed decisions that will ultimately lead to greater profitability and long-term success. By continually refining your due diligence process and staying abreast of market trends, you can ensure that you are always one step ahead of the competition, uncovering the basic real estate secrets they don't want you to know.

Never underestimate the value of due diligence. It is a powerful tool that will serve you well on your real estate journey.

Chapter 21

The Power of Market Cycles

One afternoon, as I was driving for dollars looking at properties in the streets of San Antonio, I received an unexpected call from my mentor, Armando. "Alberto," he said in his calm and reassuring voice, "I think it's time we discuss the power of market cycles and how they can impact your real estate investments."

Intrigued by the idea, I agreed to meet him later that day at a classic Tex Mex restaurant. As I took my seat across from him, Armando wasted no time in diving into the topic.

"Alberto," he began, "you've come a long way in your real estate journey, but there's still so much to learn. One of the most crucial aspects of successful investing is understanding market cycles and how they affect the value of properties. By recognizing these cycles and adapting your investment strategies accordingly, you can maximize your profits and minimize your risks."

Armando explained that the real estate market, like many other financial markets, experiences fluctuations known as market cycles. These cycles consist of four distinct phases: expansion, peak, contraction, and trough. By understanding each phase and its impact on the market, investors can make better-informed decisions and optimize their investment strategies.

Expansion. During the expansion phase, the real estate market experiences a period of growth. Demand for properties increases, leading to higher property values and a rise in construction activity. This is an excellent time for investors to identify opportunities and acquire properties that have the potential to appreciate in value.

Peak. The peak phase occurs when the market reaches its highest point of growth. Property values are at their highest, and demand may begin to plateau. Armando emphasized the importance of being cautious during this phase, as it is often followed by a period of contraction.

Contraction. As the market enters the contraction phase, demand for properties begins to decline, leading to a drop in property values. This phase can be a challenging time for investors, as it may be more difficult to sell properties or secure financing. However, Armando noted that savvy investors can find opportunities in distressed properties or by capitalizing on the reduced competition.

Trough. The trough phase represents the lowest point in the market cycle. Property values have reached their lowest point, and demand is minimal. Armando explained that while this phase can be difficult for investors, it also presents an opportunity to acquire properties at a significant discount, setting the stage for future gains as the market begins to recover.

Armando stressed the importance of staying informed about market trends and understanding how market cycles impact the value of properties. By doing so, investors can make well-informed decisions about when to buy, hold, or sell properties.

He also shared his personal approach to navigating market cycles, which involved focusing on cash flow-producing properties that could weather market fluctuations. This strategy, he said, allowed him to generate a steady stream of income, regardless of market conditions.

As our conversation drew to a close, I couldn't help but feel a newfound sense of confidence and excitement about the future of my real estate investments. Armed with the knowledge of market cycles and their impact on property values, I felt better equipped to make strategic investment decisions and uncover the basic real estate secrets they don't want you to know.

Understanding and leveraging market cycles is a critical component of successful real estate investing. By staying informed and adapting your strategies to the ever-changing market conditions, you can position yourself for long-term success and prosperity in the world of real estate.

As you embark on your own real estate investing journey, always remember the importance of understanding and leveraging market cycles. Stay informed, be adaptable, and use the knowledge of market fluctuations to your advantage.

With these principles in mind, you will be well-equipped to navigate the complexities of the market, make strategic investment decisions, and uncover the basic real estate secrets they don't want you to know. In doing so, you will unlock the potential for long-term success and prosperity in the world of real estate.

Chapter 22

Building and Maintaining Credit

I always marveled at the stories my mother used to tell me about her youth in Mexico. The tales of her adventures and life lessons always captivated my imagination. One day, she told me the story of Señor Zaragoza, the wealthy landowner from a nearby town. Señor Zaragoza was admired by many, not only for his wealth but for his keen understanding of finances and the way he managed his credit.

My mother explained to me that Señor Zaragoza was a master of credit. He understood its power and leveraged it to his advantage in building his real estate empire. This intrigued me and I decided to learn as much as I could about credit and how it could help me in my real estate endeavors.

As I delved into the world of credit, I discovered that building and maintaining good credit is one of the real estate secrets they don't want you to know. A strong credit history opens up a world of possibilities, allowing you to secure better loan terms, negotiate favorable interest rates, and access funding that might otherwise be out of reach.

The first step in building good credit is to understand the factors that influence your credit score. These include payment history, amounts owed, length of credit history, types of credit used, and new credit inquiries. By focusing on these key areas, you can work towards improving your credit standing and positioning yourself for success in the real estate world.

Making on-time payments is crucial, as it accounts for 35% of your credit score. I began by setting up automatic payments for all of my recurring expenses, ensuring that I would never miss a payment and inadvertently damage my credit score.

Credit utilization accounts for 30% of your credit score and refers to the percentage of your available credit that you're using. I learned from Señor Zaragoza's example that it's important not to overextend yourself when using credit. By keeping my balances low and paying off my debts quickly, I was able to demonstrate to lenders that I was a responsible borrower. Aim to keep your credit utilization below 30%.

The longer your credit history, the better. This factor accounts for 15% of your credit score. By having a mix of different types of credit, such as credit cards, car loans, and mortgages, I could show lenders that I was capable of managing various forms of debt responsibly.

As I continued to build my credit, I was mindful of the impact that new credit inquiries could have on my credit score. Each time you apply for credit, a hard inquiry is made on your credit report, which can temporarily lower your score. To minimize this effect, I made sure to space out my credit applications and only apply for new credit when necessary.

Throughout my journey, I learned that maintaining good credit requires diligence and persistence. By monitoring my credit reports regularly and promptly addressing any errors or discrepancies, I was able to safeguard my credit standing and protect my reputation as a responsible borrower.

As my credit score improved, I found that doors began to open for me in the world of real estate investing. I was able to secure better loan terms, negotiate lower interest rates, and access funding that allowed me to expand my real estate portfolio. The lessons I learned from Señor Zaragoza's example and my own experiences in building and maintaining good credit have proven invaluable in my journey as a real estate investor.

Building and maintaining good credit is one of the basic real estate secrets they don't want you to know. By understanding the factors that influence your credit score and taking the necessary steps to improve and protect your credit standing, you can unlock a world of opportunities in the real estate market. With persistence, dedication, and a commitment to responsible financial management, you can harness the power of credit to help you achieve your real estate investment goals.

Always remember the lessons from Señor Zaragoza and the importance of on-time payments, managing your credit utilization, and maintaining a healthy credit history. By focusing on these aspects and staying disciplined in your financial management, you can build a strong credit foundation that will serve you well in your real estate ventures.

As you continue to grow as a real estate investor, never underestimate the value of good credit and the doors it can open for you. By unlocking this basic real estate secret they don't want you to know, you can set yourself up for success and create a lasting legacy in the world of real estate.

Chapter 23

Hard Money Lenders

Alberto, bro, you've got to be kidding me, said José as he looked at me with disbelief. "Hard money lenders? Aren't they the ones who charge insane interest rates and take away your property if you don't pay them back?"

I smiled and nodded at José. "Yes, those are the ones, but let me tell you a story about the time I met a hard money lender who changed the way I saw the world of real estate financing."

I took José back to the time when I was just starting out in real estate, struggling to find a way to finance my first investment property. Banks had turned me down, and I was getting desperate.

One day, I stumbled upon a networking event for real estate investors, and there I met Eduardo, a man in his early fifties with a thick silver mustache and a wicked grin.

He had the air of someone who knew more about life and money than most people ever would.

After a brief chat, Eduardo revealed that he was a hard money lender. He told me that he could help finance my real estate project, but it would come with a catch.

"The interest rates are high, my friend," he said, leaning in closer to me. "But if you're smart and know how to use my money, you can make a fortune."

Intrigued, I decided to give it a shot. I borrowed money from Eduardo and bought a distressed property, which I then fixed up and sold for a substantial profit. I repaid the loan, and my relationship with hard money lenders began.

Over time, I learned the secrets of using hard money lenders to my advantage, and that's what I want to share with you today.

First, you must understand that hard money lenders are not the enemy. They are simply a tool in the toolbox of real estate financing. The key is to know when to use them and when to avoid them.

Hard money lenders can be a great option when you need to close a deal quickly, as they don't require the same level of documentation and red tape that banks do. They can also be more flexible with their lending terms, allowing you to structure a deal that works for you.

However, you must be careful when using hard money lenders. As José pointed out, their interest rates can be quite high, and if you're not careful, you can easily find yourself in over your head.

So, how do you use hard money lenders effectively? Follow these secrets I've learned over the years:

Leverage their speed and flexibility: When you're in a competitive market, speed is everything. A hard money loan can be the difference between securing a deal and losing it to another investor. Use this to your advantage by closing quickly and beating your competition.

Know your exit strategy: Before you even approach a hard money lender, make sure you have a clear exit strategy in place. Whether it's refinancing the property with a traditional lender or selling it for a profit, you must have a plan to repay the loan in a timely manner.

Negotiate terms: Just like any other lender, hard money lenders can be negotiated with. Don't be afraid to ask for better interest rates, fees, or loan terms. The worst they can say is no.

Build relationships: Just as I did with Eduardo, build strong relationships with your hard money lenders. They can become valuable allies in your real estate journey, providing you with insights, advice, and connections.

Keep your financial house in order: Even though hard money lenders are more lenient than traditional banks, it's still important to maintain a strong financial profile. This will make you more attractive to lenders and give you more negotiating power when discussing loan terms.

Educate yourself: Understand the ins and outs of hard money lending, including the risks and benefits. This will help you make informed decisions and ensure you're using this financing option wisely.

Use it as a stepping stone: Don't rely on hard money lenders for all your financing needs. Instead, use them as a stepping stone to build your real estate portfolio and eventually transition to more traditional financing options.

By following these secrets, you'll be able to unlock the potential of hard money lenders and use them to grow your real estate empire.

As I finished telling José my story and the lessons I'd learned, I could see a shift in his perspective.

"Alberto, I never thought of it that way," he said. "Maybe hard money lenders aren't so bad after all."

I smiled and patted him on the back. "José, my friend, remember that in real estate, knowledge is power. By understanding the tools available to you and learning how to use them effectively, you can achieve the financial freedom you've always dreamed of."

So, don't be afraid to explore the world of hard money lending. Use the secrets I've shared with you and remember, there's always more to learn in the ever-evolving world of real estate investing.

Chapter 24

Private Money Lenders

Alberto, I've been thinking about our last conversation on hard money lenders, said José, a fellow real estate investor and my dear friend. "But what about private money lenders? Aren't they a better option?"

I smiled and replied, "José, you're right. Private money lenders can be an excellent source of financing for your real estate investments. Let me tell you a story that will help you understand the difference between private money lenders and hard money lenders, and how to use them to your advantage."

I began my tale by explaining that private money lenders are individuals or groups who lend their own money to investors like us. They typically have a more personal connection with the borrower and are more flexible when it comes to loan terms and conditions. This flexibility can be a game-changer for real estate investors.

A few years ago, I met Laura, a successful entrepreneur who had recently sold her business and was looking for new investment opportunities. We struck up a conversation, and I told her about my real estate endeavors. As we spoke, I realized that Laura could be a potential private money lender for my projects.

I decided to approach her with a proposal. I showed her a rundown property that I had found, which had the potential to be a profitable fix-and-flip. Laura was intrigued but hesitant, as she had never invested in real estate before.

To ease her concerns, I shared my previous successes with her and explained how her investment would be secured by the property itself. I also offered her a better return on her money than what she was getting in her savings account.

Laura agreed to lend me the money, and we set up a win-win agreement that worked for both of us. I got the funding I needed, and she received a healthy return on her investment.

Over time, I've developed a strong relationship with Laura, and she has become one of my go-to private money lenders for my real estate deals.

Now, let me share with you the secrets I've learned about using private money lenders to finance your real estate investments:

Build relationships: Unlike hard money lenders, private money lenders are often friends, family members, or acquaintances. Therefore, it's crucial to build and maintain strong relationships with them, as trust is the foundation of these lending arrangements.

Be professional: Just because private money lenders are more flexible and informal, it doesn't mean you can be unprofessional. Present them with a well-researched and organized proposal that outlines your plans and how you intend to repay the loan.

Offer attractive terms: Private money lenders are looking for a good return on their investment. Offer them a competitive interest rate or profit-sharing arrangement that makes it worth their while to lend you their money.

Be transparent: Keep your private money lenders informed about the progress of your projects, both the successes and the challenges. Transparency builds trust and can lead to long-lasting partnerships.

Educate them: Many private money lenders may not be familiar with real estate investing. Take the time to educate them about the process and the potential benefits, so they feel more comfortable investing in your projects.

Diversify your sources: Don't rely solely on one private money lender. Cultivate relationships with multiple lenders to ensure you always have access to the funds you need.

Treat them as partners: Remember that private money lenders are investing their hard-earned money in your projects. Treat them with respect, and view them as partners in your journey to financial success.

As I finished my story, José seemed impressed. "Alberto, it sounds like private money lenders are a fantastic resource. I'll definitely start looking for potential lenders in my network."

I nodded in agreement. "José, remember that real estate investing is all about leveraging resources, and private money lenders can be a powerful ally in your quest for financial freedom. By nurturing relationships, being professional, and treating them as partners, you can unlock the true potential of private money lending."

José nodded, clearly inspired. "Thanks for sharing your experience and insights, Alberto. I can see now how private money lenders can play a crucial role in my real estate journey."

As we parted ways, I knew that José had gained valuable knowledge that would serve him well in his real estate investing endeavors. And, I hope that you too can take these lessons to heart and use private money lenders to propel your real estate dreams to new heights.

Chapter 25

OPM - Other People's Money

As I sat down with my friend, Kyle, I could see that he was frustrated. "Alberto, I just don't get it. How do you find the money to finance all your real estate deals? I don't have a fortune lying around to invest in properties."

I smiled and replied, "Kyle, my friend, you're looking at it the wrong way. You don't need a fortune of your own to invest in real estate. You just need to learn how to use OPM - Other People's Money."

Kyle looked at me with a puzzled expression. "OPM? What do you mean?"

I leaned back in my chair and began to tell Kyle the story of how I first learned the power of using other people's money to invest in real estate.

A few years back, I attended a real estate seminar where I met an experienced investor named Eduardo. He had been investing in properties for years, and his portfolio was impressive. As we talked, he told me the secret to his success: he never used his own money to finance his deals.

At first, I didn't believe him. But as he explained the concept of OPM, I began to understand the potential it held for real estate investors like myself.

Eduardo taught me that by leveraging other people's money, I could invest in properties I otherwise wouldn't have been able to afford. This would allow me to grow my portfolio faster and achieve financial freedom sooner.

Over the years, I've used OPM to finance countless real estate deals, and now I want to share with you the secrets I've learned about using other people's money to fund your investments:

Partner with others: Find investors who are willing to put up the money for your deals in exchange for a share of the profits. This can be family members, friends, or even business associates. Just be sure to have a clear agreement in place that outlines the terms of the partnership.

Use hard money and private money lenders: As I've discussed in previous chapters, hard money and private money lenders can be a fantastic source of financing for your real estate deals. By leveraging their funds, you can invest in properties without putting up your own money.

Seller financing: In some cases, property owners are willing to finance the sale of their property themselves. This can be an attractive option for investors, as it often involves more favorable terms and lower interest rates than traditional bank loans.

Creative financing strategies: There are numerous creative financing strategies that can help you use other people's money to fund your real estate investments. These can include lease options, subject-to deals, and more. Be sure to educate yourself on these methods and use them wisely.

Network: The more people you know in the real estate industry, the more opportunities you'll have to find financing for your deals. Attend networking events, join real estate investment groups, and connect with others in the field to discover new sources of funding.

As I finished sharing my secrets with Kyle, I could see the lightbulb go off in his head. "Alberto, I never thought of it that way. I've been so focused on using my own money that I didn't realize all the other options available to me."

I grinned and said. "Kyle, remember that real estate investing is all about leveraging resources, and one of the most powerful resources you have is other people's money. By learning how to use OPM effectively, you can propel your real estate investing journey to new heights."

So, don't be afraid to use other people's money to fund your real estate investments. By understanding the power of OPM and utilizing the strategies I've shared with you, you can unlock the potential of this powerful tool and achieve the financial freedom you've always dreamed of.

As Kyle left our meeting, I knew he was on his way to a brighter future in real estate investing. With newfound knowledge and determination, he was ready to embrace the power of OPM and create a lasting legacy for himself and his family.

I hope that you too can take these lessons to heart and use other people's money to fuel your real estate dreams.

Remember, knowledge is power, and the more you know, the more successful you'll be in the world of real estate investing.

Chapter 26

OPE - Other People's Experience

One afternoon, I found myself in a conversation with my longtime friend, Sofia. She was an aspiring real estate investor, eager to learn the secrets of success in the industry. "Alberto, I've read countless books and attended numerous seminars, but I still feel like I have so much to learn. How can I speed up the learning process?"

Remembering my own early days in real estate investing. "Sofia, I have a secret for you. The key to accelerating your growth as a real estate investor is to learn from OPE - Other People's Experience."

Sofia raised her eyebrows in curiosity. "OPE? Tell me more."

I began my tale by recounting my first encounter with the concept of OPE. Back when I started my real estate journey, I met an older investor named Tony. He had been investing in properties for decades and had accumulated a wealth of knowledge and experience. As we spoke, I realized that learning from Tony's experience could save me years of trial and error.

I asked Tony if he would be willing to mentor me, and he graciously agreed. Over the years, our mentor-mentee relationship blossomed, and I soaked up every bit of wisdom that Tony had to offer. By learning from his experience, I was able to avoid costly mistakes and make smarter decisions in my own investing journey.

I explained to Sofia that leveraging OPE is like standing on the shoulders of giants. By learning from those who have gone before us, we can reach heights we never thought possible.

Now, let me share with you the secrets I've learned about using other people's experience to fast-track your real estate investing success:

Find a mentor: Seek out experienced investors who are willing to share their knowledge and insights with you. A mentor can provide invaluable guidance and help you navigate the complex world of real estate investing.

Join a mastermind group: Surround yourself with like-minded individuals who are also pursuing real estate success. A mastermind group can be a source of inspiration, support, and shared learning.

Attend networking events: Make it a point to attend real estate conferences, workshops, and local investor meetups. These events are excellent opportunities to learn from seasoned investors and make valuable connections.

Read books and articles: Never underestimate the power of the written word. Many successful real estate investors have shared their experience and insights in books and articles. Devour these resources to absorb their wisdom.

Listen to podcasts and watch videos: The digital age has made it easier than ever to access the expertise of others. Podcasts and videos can be a goldmine of information and inspiration from seasoned real estate investors.

Ask questions: Don't be afraid to ask questions when you're interacting with experienced investors. They've likely faced the same challenges you're encountering and can offer valuable advice based on their own experiences.

Learn from your own experiences: While it's essential to learn from other people's experiences, don't forget to reflect on your own journey. Each deal and situation you encounter will teach you valuable lessons that will help shape your future success.

As I finished sharing my secrets, Sofia's eyes sparkled with excitement. "Alberto, I never thought of it that way. Leveraging other people's experience seems like a surefire way to accelerate my growth as a real estate investor."

"Sofia, remember that no one achieves success in real estate investing overnight. But by tapping into the wisdom and experience of others, you can shorten your learning curve and make your journey to financial freedom that much smoother."

I encourage you to embrace the power of OPE in your real estate investing journey. Learn from the experience of others, surround yourself with knowledgeable mentors and peers, and never stop seeking new sources of wisdom. By leveraging other people's experience, you can accelerate your growth and achieve the financial freedom you've always dreamed of.

As Sofia and I parted ways, I knew she was on the right path to success in real estate investing. With newfound determination and a thirst for knowledge, she was ready to unlock the power of OPE and create a lasting legacy for herself and her family.

Take these lessons and use other people's experience to fuel your real estate dreams.

Chapter 27

OPT - Other People's Time

One evening, I found myself at a local real estate investors' gathering, chatting with my good friend, Allan. A dedicated investor, but Allan had a dilemma: "Alberto, I'm struggling to manage my time effectively. There are so many aspects to real estate investing, and I feel like I can't do everything on my own."

I replied, "Allan, you're not alone in feeling that way. One of the most important lessons I've learned in my real estate journey is the power of leveraging OPT - Other People's Time."

Allan looked intrigued. "OPT? How can other people's time help me succeed in real estate investing?"

I began my story by recalling a crucial turning point in my own real estate career. I had just started acquiring rental properties, and I was trying to manage everything on my own. Between finding tenants, dealing with maintenance issues, and managing the financial side of things, I was quickly becoming overwhelmed.

That's when I met Carlos, an experienced property manager. He introduced me to the concept of OPT and showed me how hiring a property manager could free up my time, allowing me to focus on finding new deals and expanding my real estate portfolio.

By leveraging Carlos's time and expertise, I was able to grow my business and achieve a level of success I never thought possible.

I shared with Allan the valuable lessons I've learned about using other people's time to grow your real estate investing business:

Build a team: Real estate investing is a team sport. Surround yourself with knowledgeable and experienced professionals, such as real estate agents, property managers, contractors, and attorneys. By leveraging their time and expertise, you can focus on what you do best - finding and closing deals.

Delegate: It's essential to learn how to delegate tasks to others, especially as your real estate portfolio grows. Identify your strengths and weaknesses, and delegate tasks that fall outside your areas of expertise. This will not only save you time but also ensure that each task is handled by someone with the appropriate skills and knowledge.

Hire a virtual assistant: As your real estate business expands, you may find that administrative tasks begin to eat into your time. Hiring a virtual assistant can help you stay organized and manage your day-to-day tasks more efficiently.

Automate processes: Embrace technology and use tools and software that can help you automate time-consuming tasks, such as tracking expenses, managing your properties, and communicating with your team.

Outsource: If a task is too specialized or time-consuming, consider outsourcing it to a professional. For example, hiring an accountant or bookkeeper to handle your finances can free up your time to focus on growing your real estate portfolio.

Focus on high-value activities: Identify the activities that bring the most value to your business and prioritize your time accordingly. By concentrating on high-value tasks, you can achieve maximum results with minimum time investment.

As I finished sharing my insights, I could see Allan's eyes light up with understanding. "Alberto, you've opened my eyes to the power of leveraging other people's time. I can see how this will help me manage my time more effectively and grow my real estate business."

Remember that the key to success in real estate investing is not just working harder, but also working smarter. By leveraging other people's time, you can focus on the tasks that matter most and achieve your goals faster."

So, I encourage you to harness the power of OPT in your real estate investing journey. Learn to build a team, delegate tasks, and use technology to your advantage. By leveraging other people's time, you can achieve the financial freedom you've always dreamed of.

Chapter 28

Land and Development

Land is the only thing in the world worth working for, worth fighting for, worth dying for, because it's the only thing that lasts. These were the words in the movie "Gone with the Wind" that echoed in my mind as I looked out across the acres of land I had just acquired. It wasn't much to look at in its current state, but I knew that with time and effort, this land would be the foundation of my wealth. This chapter is dedicated to the importance of land and development in the world of real estate, as well as the lessons I've learned from my experiences.

It all began when I met Señor Uribe, a seasoned real estate investor in his late 60s who had a gift for seeing potential in the most unexpected places. Señor Uribe was known for turning seemingly worthless plots of land into thriving communities, and I was eager to learn his secrets. He invited me to accompany him on a trip to inspect a new piece of land he had just acquired. As we drove towards the location, I noticed the landscape becoming increasingly barren, and I couldn't help but wonder what he saw in such a desolate place.

As we reached our destination, I noticed that the land itself was nothing more than a dusty, undeveloped expanse of brush and weeds. It was hard for me to imagine anyone wanting to live there. Sensing my skepticism, Señor Uribe chuckled and said, "Alberto, my boy, you must learn to see beyond what is in front of you. This land may not look like much now, but it has potential. All it needs is a little vision and some hard work."

He went on to explain that by developing the land into a thriving community, he would be creating something of value that people would want to be a part of. "You see, Alberto, the value of land is not in what it is, but in what it can become. Development is the key to unlocking its true potential."

Over the next few months, I watched as Señor Uribe meticulously planned and executed the development of the land. He started by securing the necessary permits and approvals, which allowed him to begin construction on the infrastructure that would support the new community. Roads, water, and electricity were installed, transforming the barren land into a habitable space. As the infrastructure took shape, the value of the land increased significantly.

Next, Señor Uribe focused on building homes and commercial spaces, creating a diverse mix of properties that would attract a wide range of tenants and buyers. He carefully considered the needs and desires of the target market, ensuring that the properties would be in high demand. As the community began to take shape, the value of the land continued to grow.

Through this experience, I learned several important lessons about land and development. First, I realized that the true value of land lies in its potential for development. An undeveloped plot of land might not seem like much on the surface, but with the right vision and effort, it can be transformed into a valuable asset. Second, I learned that development requires both patience and persistence. It can take time and hard work to turn a piece of land into a thriving community, but the rewards can be well worth the effort.

Finally, I discovered the importance of understanding the needs and desires of the target market. By building properties that appeal to a wide range of buyers and tenants, you can create a community that is in high demand, further increasing the value of the land.

As I stood on the now bustling streets of the community that Señor Uribe had built, I marveled at the transformation that had taken place. The once barren land had become a thriving, valuable asset, and I knew that I had learned a valuable lesson about the power of land and development. I was grateful for the wisdom and guidance that Señor Uribe had shared with me, and I was eager to apply these lessons to my own real estate investments.

In the years since my time with Señor Uribe, I have followed in his footsteps, acquiring and developing land in various locations. Each new project has brought its own unique challenges and opportunities, but the lessons I learned from Señor Uribe have remained constant. Through hard work, vision, and persistence, I have been able to transform once-forgotten parcels of land into valuable real estate assets, providing both financial security and a sense of accomplishment.

As you venture into the world of real estate, I encourage you to keep the lessons of this chapter in mind. Don't be afraid to seek out undeveloped land and imagine the possibilities that lie beneath the surface.

Remember that development is the key to unlocking the true potential of land, and that with patience, persistence, and an understanding of the target market, you can create thriving communities that contribute to your wealth and success.

Chapter 29

Investing in AirBNB Properties

One early morning, I found myself sitting in a small café sipping on a cappuccino, enjoying a brief respite from my hectic schedule. As I people-watched, I noticed a diverse group of tourists strolling by young backpackers, families with children, and even a few elderly couples all exploring the city with excitement in their eyes. It was then that I realized the enormous potential that lay in the emerging market of short-term rentals, especially with the growing popularity of platforms like Airbnb.

It wasn't long before I sought the guidance of my good friend and mentor, Armando, who had already dabbled in Airbnb investments. We met at a charming, bohemian-style Airbnb rental that he owned in the heart of San Antonio. The place was immaculate and tastefully decorated, creating a warm and inviting atmosphere for its guests.

"Alberto," Armando said with a glint in his eye, "investing in Airbnb properties is an entirely different ball game compared to traditional real estate investments. It requires a different approach, but the rewards can be quite substantial."

As we toured the property, he shared his insights and experiences about investing in Airbnb properties. Here are the lessons that I learned from him, which have since become an integral part of my own real estate investment strategy.

Location, Location, Location: The first rule of real estate investing still applies to Airbnb properties. Armando emphasized that a prime location is crucial for attracting guests and maintaining high occupancy rates. Look for properties in popular tourist destinations, near landmarks, or in trendy neighborhoods with easy access to public transportation and local amenities.

Cater to Your Target Market: Understanding the needs and desires of your potential guests is key to running a successful Airbnb rental. Armando's property, for example, was specifically designed to appeal to tourists seeking a cozy, authentic experience in the heart of San Antonio. He carefully selected furnishings, artwork, and amenities that would make his guests feel right at home while still offering them a unique, memorable stay.

Quality Matters: Armando stressed the importance of maintaining a high standard of cleanliness and quality in your Airbnb rental. A well maintained property with modern amenities and thoughtful touches will not only attract more bookings but also encourage positive reviews, which are essential for success on the platform.

Be a Great Host: In the world of Airbnb, being a great host is just as important as owning a great property. Armando hired a management team to be attentive and responsive to his guests, offering local tips and recommendations, and even providing a welcome basket with snacks and local delicacies. By going the extra mile, he was able to build a loyal clientele and ensure a steady stream of bookings.

Treat It as a Business: Lastly, Armando emphasized that to truly succeed in the Airbnb market, one must treat it as a business rather than a hobby. This means keeping accurate records, managing expenses, and constantly seeking ways to improve your property and guest experience.

As I began to implement these lessons in my own Airbnb investments, I found that they held the keys to success in this new and exciting market. By carefully selecting prime locations, catering to the needs of my guests, maintaining high quality properties, and providing exceptional hospitality, I was able to generate a significant income stream and further diversify my real estate portfolio.

Investing in Airbnb properties can be a lucrative addition to your real estate investment strategy. By understanding the unique dynamics of the short-term rental market and applying the lessons shared by Armando, you too can unlock the secrets to success in this rapidly growing industry. Keep an open mind, adapt to the ever changing landscape, and always strive to provide the best possible experience for your guests as you embark on this new journey.

As you navigate the world of Airbnb property investments, remember the valuable lessons shared by Armando and the experiences that have shaped your own understanding of the market. By staying committed to excellence in every aspect of your Airbnb business, from the location and design of your properties to the quality of your guest experience, you will build a strong foundation for long-term success.

Embrace the challenges and rewards that come with investing in Airbnb properties and continue to learn, adapt, and grow as both an investor and a host. By doing so, you will not only create a profitable income stream but also contribute to the vibrant and diverse world of short-term rentals, making unforgettable experiences possible for travelers from all walks of life.

In the end, the true secrets of success in Airbnb property investments lie in your dedication, passion, and willingness to go the extra mile for your guests.

Chapter 30

Maintenance and Repairs

It was a rainy afternoon in San Antonio when I received a frantic call from one of my tenants, who informed me that a pipe had burst, causing water to gush out and flood the entire place. I could hear the panic in her voice, and I knew that I needed to act fast to prevent further damage to the property. This experience served as a stark reminder of the importance of maintenance and repairs in the world of real estate investing.

I quickly called my trusted contractor, Luis, who had been my go to resource for all things related to property maintenance and repairs. Over the years, Luis had become a close friend and project manager, sharing his wealth of knowledge on how to properly maintain and repair my properties. As we assessed the damage from the burst pipe, I realized that this unfortunate incident offered valuable lessons in property management that I could share with others.

Prevention is Key: Luis explained that regular maintenance is crucial for preventing costly repairs and ensuring the longevity of your properties. He advised me to create a maintenance schedule for each property, including routine checks for plumbing, electrical systems, and HVAC units. By keeping up with regular maintenance, you can often catch small issues before they become big, expensive problems.

Build a Reliable Network: Having a reliable network of professionals, like Luis, can be a lifesaver when it comes to property maintenance and repairs. Establish relationships with trusted contractors, plumbers, electricians, and other service providers who can respond quickly and effectively to emergencies. By cultivating these connections, you can ensure that your properties are well-maintained and your tenants are well-cared for.

Set Aside Funds for Repairs: As a real estate investor, it is important to set aside a portion of your income for property maintenance and repairs. Luis suggested creating a dedicated reserve fund that can be used to address any unexpected issues that arise. This will not only provide you with peace of mind but also protect your long-term investment.

Communicate with Your Tenants: A key component of successful property management is maintaining open lines of communication with your tenants. Encourage them to report any maintenance issues promptly, and be responsive to their concerns. By addressing problems quickly and efficiently, you can create a positive living environment for your tenants and minimize the risk of damage to your property.

Stay Informed on Building Codes and Regulations: Luis emphasized the importance of staying up-to-date on local building codes and regulations. This knowledge can help you ensure that your properties are in compliance with safety standards, preventing potential fines and legal issues. It also allows you to make informed decisions when it comes to property upgrades and improvements.

As I worked alongside Luis to repair the damage caused by the burst pipe, I was grateful for the lessons he had shared with me. These insights have not only helped me maintain my properties more effectively but have also saved me a great deal of time, money, and stress.

Proper maintenance and repairs are essential components of successful real estate investing. By prioritizing prevention, building a reliable network, setting aside funds for repairs, communicating with your tenants, and staying informed on building codes and regulations, you can protect your investments and maximize their value.

Remember, a well-maintained property is not only more attractive to potential tenants and buyers but also more likely to appreciate in value over time. By applying the lessons in this chapter, you can unlock the secrets to property management success and ensure the long-term profitability of your real estate investments.

Chapter 31

Property comps

I still remember the day when I stumbled upon a seemingly perfect real estate investment opportunity. It was a quaint, well-maintained house in a desirable neighborhood with a price tag that seemed too good to be true. Excited by the prospect, I immediately called my mentor, Tom, a seasoned real estate investor, to share my findings.

Tom listened carefully as I excitedly recounted the details of the property, and then calmly said, "Alberto, before you make any decisions, you must first understand the property comps in the area. That's the only way to truly know if this is a good investment."

Intrigued by his words, I asked Tom to explain the concept of property comps and how they could help me in my real estate investing journey. He agreed to meet me at a local down town steakhouse to share his wisdom, and here are the lessons I learned from him that day.

Understanding Property Comps: Tom explained that property comps, short for comparables, are recently sold or listed properties similar to the one you're considering for investment. They help determine the fair market value of a property by comparing it to similar properties in the same area, taking into account factors like size, age, condition, and location.

Gathering Accurate Comps: To gather accurate property comps, Tom advised me to focus on properties that have sold within the past six months and are located within a mile of the property I was considering. Additionally, he suggested using online resources like real estate websites and local multiple listing services (MLS) to find relevant data.

Analyzing Comps: Once you have gathered a list of comps, Tom emphasized the importance of analyzing the data to determine the property's true value. He suggested looking for trends in the data, such as whether prices are increasing or decreasing, and adjusting the value of the property accordingly.

Making Adjustments: Tom pointed out that no two properties are exactly alike, so it's essential to make adjustments for any differences between the property you're considering and the comps. For example, if your property has a larger lot size or an additional bedroom, you would adjust the value upwards. Conversely, if the property is in worse condition or has fewer amenities, you would adjust the value downwards.

The Importance of Timing: Tom also emphasized the importance of timing when it comes to property comps. He explained that real estate markets can be cyclical, and it's crucial to consider how the current market conditions might impact the property's value. By understanding market trends, you can make better decisions on when to buy or sell a property.

Using Comps in Negotiations: Armed with the knowledge of property comps, you can use this information to your advantage during negotiations. Tom explained that by presenting accurate comps to sellers, you can justify your offer and potentially secure a better deal.

Learning from Comps: Finally, Tom suggested that property comps can serve as an invaluable learning tool for real estate investors. By regularly analyzing comps, you can gain a deeper understanding of your local market and identify trends that can help you make smarter investment decisions.

Following our conversation, I eagerly applied the lessons I learned from Tom to the property I was considering. As I analyzed the comps, I discovered that the property was indeed undervalued, and I was able to negotiate a favorable purchase price.

Understanding and utilizing property comps is an essential skill for any real estate investor. By gathering accurate data, analyzing trends, making adjustments, and using comps in negotiations, you can make informed investment decisions and maximize the potential return on your investments.

Remember, in the world of real estate investing, knowledge is power. By mastering the art of property comps, you can unlock the secrets to successful property valuations and ensure that you're making the right moves to build your real estate empire. The lessons shared by Tom will not only help you accurately assess the value of potential investments but also provide you with a deeper understanding of your local market, enabling you to make strategic decisions that contribute to your long-term success.

So, as you continue your journey in real estate investing, remember to always prioritize the importance of property comps. By doing so, you'll gain invaluable insights into the market and develop a keen eye for identifying lucrative opportunities. With dedication, perseverance, and the application of these lessons, you can unlock the secrets of successful property valuations and ultimately build a thriving real estate portfolio.

Chapter 32

Marketing and Advertising

After a few successful real estate investments under my belt, I found myself eager to take on a new challenge. I purchased a charming property that I was certain would attract tenants easily. However, weeks went by, and the property remained vacant. Feeling disheartened, I turned to my friend, Nicole, a marketing and advertising expert, for guidance.

Nicole explained that even the most appealing properties can remain unnoticed without the right marketing and advertising strategies. She shared her insights on the essential steps for effectively promoting my real estate investments, and here are the key lessons I learned that day.

Know Your Target Audience: Nicole emphasized the importance of understanding the demographics and preferences of my target audience. She advised me to consider factors such as age, income, family size, and lifestyle when creating marketing materials. By tailoring my message to resonate with the right audience, I could increase the chances of attracting potential tenants or buyers.

Create a Strong Brand: To make my property stand out in a competitive market, Nicole suggested building a strong brand that would be easily recognizable and memorable. She advised me to develop a consistent color scheme, logo, and tagline that represented the unique characteristics of my property. By establishing a strong brand, I could create a lasting impression on potential tenants or buyers.

Utilize Multiple Channels: Nicole recommended using a variety of marketing channels to reach my target audience. She suggested a mix of online and offline methods, such as listing my property on popular real estate websites, creating engaging social media content, and distributing eye-catching flyers in the local community. By leveraging multiple channels, I could increase my property's visibility and reach a broader audience.

High-Quality Visuals: Nicole stressed the importance of high-quality visuals in showcasing my property's best features. She recommended hiring a professional photographer to capture stunning images and even suggested creating a virtual tour to give potential tenants or buyers a more immersive experience. By investing in high-quality visuals, I could effectively highlight my property's unique selling points.

Craft Compelling Descriptions: To pique the interest of potential tenants or buyers, Nicole advised me to create compelling property descriptions that emphasized the benefits of living in my property. She suggested focusing on the property's unique features, such as its location, amenities, or recent upgrades. By crafting captivating descriptions, I could entice potential tenants or buyers to take a closer look.

Build a Positive Reputation: Nicole reminded me that word-of-mouth marketing is still one of the most powerful forms of advertising. She encouraged me to maintain open communication with my tenants, address their concerns promptly, and request reviews or testimonials from satisfied tenants or buyers. By fostering a positive reputation, I could attract new tenants or buyers through referrals and recommendations.

Taking Nicole's advice to heart, I implemented the marketing and advertising strategies we had discussed. Within a short period, I began to see a significant increase in interest in my property, and soon enough, I had secured a tenant.

In conclusion, effective marketing and advertising are critical components of successful real estate investing. By understanding your target audience, building a strong brand, utilizing multiple channels, investing in high-quality visuals, crafting compelling descriptions, and fostering a positive reputation, you can attract potential tenants or buyers and maximize your property's potential.

Remember, even the most impressive real estate investments can fall short without the right marketing and advertising strategies. By applying the lessons shared by Nicole, you can unlock the secrets to showcasing your properties and building a thriving real estate portfolio.

Chapter 33

Exit Strategies

Growing up in a Hispanic family, I remember my mother and grandfather talking about the importance of working hard and owning a home. They believed that owning a home was the ultimate symbol of success and a surefire way to build wealth.

Years later, as a successful real estate investor, I've realized that there's more to real estate than just owning a home. There are countless ways to generate wealth through real estate, and one of the most important aspects of any real estate investment is knowing when and how to exit.

In my previous chapters, I shared with you some of the "Basic Real Estate Secrets They Don't Want You to Know." I've talked about how to find the right deals, negotiate the best terms, and manage your properties efficiently. But now, it's time to discuss the final piece of the puzzle: the exit strategy.

An exit strategy is your plan for cashing out of an investment and reaping the benefits of your hard work. It's the moment when you turn your paper profits into real money. And just like my mother and grandfather taught me, it's crucial to have a plan.

Flipping Properties. One of the most popular exit strategies for real estate investors is flipping properties. Flipping involves buying a property, making improvements, and then selling it for a profit within a short period. This strategy works best in a rising market, where property values are increasing rapidly.

If you decide to flip a property, make sure to do your due diligence. Estimate the costs of repairs and improvements, and factor in the holding costs, such as taxes, insurance, and interest on your loan. Keep in mind that the quicker you can flip the property, the better your profit margins will be.

Refinancing is another popular exit strategy that allows you to extract equity from your property without selling it. By refinancing your mortgage, you can access the increased value of your property and use the funds to invest in other opportunities or improve your existing property.

Keep in mind that refinancing comes with costs, such as closing fees and interest payments, so make sure to weigh the benefits against the costs before making a decision.

Lease Options. A lease option is an agreement that gives the tenant the right to purchase the property at a predetermined price within a specific time frame. This can be a great exit strategy for investors who want to lock in a profit but are willing to wait for the tenant to exercise their option to buy.

When entering into a lease option agreement, make sure to set a purchase price that factors in potential appreciation and negotiate favorable terms that protect your interests.

Seller Financing is an exit strategy where the investor acts as the bank, lending money to the buyer to purchase the property. This can be an attractive option for investors who want to cash out of their property but are unable to find a traditional buyer.

By offering seller financing, you can potentially attract more buyers and negotiate a higher sale price. However, keep in mind that there are risks involved, such as the buyer defaulting on the loan or damaging the property. To mitigate these risks, make sure to thoroughly vet potential buyers, set appropriate interest rates, and secure a substantial down payment.

1031 Exchange. A 1031 exchange is a tax-deferred exit strategy that allows investors to swap one investment property for another without incurring capital gains taxes. By utilizing a 1031 exchange, you can leverage the equity from your existing property to purchase a more valuable property, ultimately growing your real estate portfolio and deferring taxes on your gains.

To take advantage of a 1031 exchange, it's essential to follow strict IRS guidelines, such as identifying a like-kind replacement property within 45 days and closing on the new property within 180 days. Consulting with a tax professional or a qualified intermediary can help ensure you navigate this process correctly.

Wholesaling is an exit strategy where an investor secures a property under contract and then assigns or sells the contract to another investor for a fee. This can be an attractive option for those looking to make quick profits without actually owning or managing the property.

If you decide to wholesale a property, make sure to build a solid network of potential buyers and have a clear understanding of the property's value and potential improvements. Your goal is to find deals with enough profit margin for both you and the end investor.

Knowing when and how to exit your real estate investments is just as important as knowing how to acquire and manage them. Having a clear exit strategy in place will allow you to make informed decisions and maximize your profits.

Chapter 34

Commercial Wholesaling

As I strolled down the bustling streets of San Antonio, the hum of conversation and the rhythmic sounds of Fiesta music filled the air. A neon sign caught my attention, casting a warm glow on the sleek glass windows of a commercial building. My mind wandered to the topic of commercial wholesaling and how it has transformed my real estate journey.

Years ago, my mentor Tom, a savvy and astute businessman, invited me to lunch at his favorite steak house in the heart of San Antonio. As the server brought our steaks, he leaned in closer and whispered, "Alberto, I'm about to reveal a secret that will change the way you approach real estate." Intrigued, I listened intently as Tom introduced me to the world of commercial wholesaling.

"Commercial wholesaling," he explained, "is a strategy used to connect commercial property sellers with potential buyers without actually taking ownership of the property.

It's a low-risk, high-reward method of investing that has made many savvy investors, like myself, wealthy."

He continued, "The key is to find commercial properties at a discounted price, secure them under contract, and then quickly assign the contract to an end buyer for a profit." As we discussed the nuances of commercial wholesaling, I began to understand that this strategy was truly one of the best-kept secrets in the real estate industry.

My journey into commercial wholesaling began with research. I spent countless hours poring over books, attending seminars, and conversing with experienced investors like Tom. Each time I gleaned a nugget of wisdom, my passion for real estate investing grew stronger.

One sunny afternoon, I met with a local real estate agent who specialized in commercial properties. "In commercial wholesaling," she said, "you'll need to build a solid network of buyers and sellers. A well-connected investor is unstoppable in this game."

Taking her advice to heart, I began to attend networking events and forged relationships with like-minded individuals. I even connected with other wholesalers who were eager to share their experiences and collaborate on deals.

As my network grew, so did my opportunities. I soon found a commercial property that was ripe for wholesaling–a distressed office building in a prime location. The owner was eager to sell, and I negotiated a favorable contract. With my newfound connections, I was able to quickly find an investor who was interested in purchasing the property.

On the day of the closing, I felt a mixture of excitement and anxiety. As the end buyer signed the final papers, I realized that I had successfully completed my first commercial wholesale deal. Tom's secret had opened up a world of possibilities for me, and I was eager to continue exploring this lucrative strategy.

Commercial wholesaling has since become an integral part of my real estate investing career. I've closed numerous deals, and my network of buyers and sellers has expanded exponentially. With each transaction, I've learned valuable lessons and honed my skills as a real estate investor.

In sharing my journey, I hope to inspire others to explore the world of commercial wholesaling. The opportunities are endless for those who are willing to put in the effort and develop their networks. As Tom once said, "The key to success in real estate is to always be learning, always be growing, and never be afraid to pursue new strategies."

So, my fellow investors, I encourage you to step out of your comfort zone and delve into the realm of commercial wholesaling. Who knows? It just might be the secret that catapults you to real estate success. And always remember, there are countless "Basic Real Estate Secrets They Don't Want You to Know" waiting to be discovered.

As I continued my stroll through the busy streets, the neon sign now a fading memory, I smiled, knowing that I had unlocked one of the most powerful secrets in the real estate industry.

The vibrant city of San Antonio, with its rich culture and thriving business landscape, had become the perfect backdrop for my commercial wholesaling ventures. And with the guidance of my mentor, Tom, I was well on my way to forging a successful career in real estate investing.

Chapter 35

Tax Strategies for Real Estate Investors

I t was a hot summer day, and I was sitting across from my accountant, staring at a pile of paperwork on his desk. I dreaded the thought of having to pay the exorbitant taxes on my real estate investments. However, my accountant, who was also a seasoned real estate investor, leaned over and said, "Alberto, there are ways to legally minimize your taxes and maximize your profits."

I leaned forward, eager to hear his advice. He began to explain the various tax strategies that real estate investors use to minimize their tax burden. "One of the most powerful strategies," he said, "is the use of depreciation. Depreciation is the process of deducting the cost of your property over a number of years. This means that you can offset your rental income with deductions for depreciation and other expenses, reducing your overall tax liability."

He also mentioned the benefits of investing in a real estate IRA, which allows investors to defer taxes on their earnings until they withdraw the funds in retirement. "By investing in a real estate IRA," he explained, "you can build wealth while minimizing your taxes and securing your financial future."

As I left my accountant's office, I realized that I had only scratched the surface of the many tax strategies available to real estate investors. I began to research the topic further, poring over books and attending seminars to expand my knowledge.

One day, I met a successful real estate investor named Robert at a networking event. As we chatted, he mentioned that he had implemented a tax strategy called cost segregation. "Cost segregation is a process," he said, "where you break down the components of your property into shorter depreciable lives, allowing you to take larger tax deductions upfront."

I was fascinated by this strategy and began to research it further. Cost segregation allowed me to reclassify certain components of my properties, such as carpets, appliances, and lighting fixtures, as personal property, which can be depreciated over a shorter time frame than the building itself. This allowed me to take larger tax deductions upfront and increase my overall cash flow.

Another tax strategy that I discovered was the 1031 exchange. This strategy allowed me to defer paying taxes on the profits from the sale of one property by using the proceeds to purchase another property of equal or greater value. By doing so, I was able to continue building my real estate portfolio while minimizing my tax liability.

As I continued to explore the world of tax strategies for real estate investors, I realized that there were countless opportunities to legally minimize my tax burden and increase my overall profitability. The key was to stay informed and educated, constantly seeking out new strategies and opportunities.

And with the right tax strategies in place, real estate investors like you can achieve financial freedom and build generational wealth. By minimizing your tax liability, you can reinvest your profits back into your real estate portfolio, allowing you to grow your wealth and expand your businesses.

Take the time to learn about tax strategies for real estate investors. Seek out the advice of experienced professionals like my accountant and Robert, and stay up-to-date on the latest tax laws and regulations. By doing so, you can ensure that you are maximizing your profits and minimizing your tax liability, paving the way for a successful and prosperous future in real estate investing.

Remember, there are always "Basic Real Estate Secrets They Don't Want You to Know" waiting to be discovered, and tax strategies for real estate investors are one of the most powerful secrets of all. So don't wait, start implementing these strategies today and watch as your real estate portfolio grows and your wealth expands.

Chapter 36

Investing in a Changing Economy

As I sat and open my laptop to check my emails, I couldn't help but admire the ever evolving cityscape outside the window. The thought struck me that change is truly the only constant in life, and this rings especially true when considering the economy.

When I first dipped my toes into the world of real estate investing, I quickly realized that the economy played a crucial role in the success of my ventures. To truly excel in this field, one must learn to adapt and make intelligent decisions in the face of economic flows.

In my journey, I've been blessed with two influential mentors. The first, whom I'll call Armando, was a prosperous real estate investor. The second, my loving mother, was a cautious woman who found comfort in the security of a stable job and a predictable income. Each of them imparted valuable lessons to me, and their contrasting viewpoints helped shape my understanding of money and investing.

One rainy afternoon, Armando invited me to join him on a visit to one of his properties. As we strolled through the neighborhood, I observed that many of the homes bore striking similarities to one another. I inquired whether this was advantageous or disadvantageous. With a chuckle, Armando replied, "It's neither good nor bad. It's simply a reflection of the times."

He proceeded to explain that during economic upswings, new houses are typically constructed rapidly and often boast similar designs. Conversely, during economic downturns, construction projects decelerate, and the housing market becomes increasingly competitive. "The economy resembles the seasons," he said. "There are periods of growth and periods of stagnation, and as an investor, you must learn to adapt to these shifts."

My mother, on the other hand, perceived the economy from a different angle. She believed that investing in real estate was too perilous, particularly during times of uncertainty. The safety of a secure job and fixed income was her preference. "Why gamble with your hard earned money?" she would often caution.

Despite their opposing stances, both Armando and my mother raised valid points. I understood that to be a successful real estate investor, I needed to strike a balance between their two perspectives.

So, how does one invest in a changing economy? Here are several lessons I've gathered from my experiences:

Diversify your investments: Avoid putting all your eggs in one basket. Distribute your investments among various types of properties and locations to help mitigate the risks associated with economic fluctuations.

Stay informed: Keep abreast of market trends, government policies, and other factors that could impact the real estate market. This will enable you to make better informed decisions and adapt to changes more effectively.

Be proactive: Successful investors are always on the lookout for new opportunities. Stay active in your local real estate community, attend seminars, and network with other investors to learn about up-and-coming neighborhoods and potential deals.

Focus on cash flow: Prioritize properties that generate positive cash flow over those that merely promise appreciation. This can provide you with a consistent income stream, irrespective of market conditions.

Practice due diligence: Don't rush into investments or make impulsive decisions. Diligently analyze each opportunity and ensure it aligns with your financial objectives and risk tolerance.

Leverage your network: Surround yourself with knowledgeable individuals, such as real estate agents, property managers, and fellow investors. They can offer invaluable insights and help you navigate the ever-changing landscape of real estate investing.

Develop an adaptable mindset: The ability to adapt to changes in the economy is crucial for long-term success in real estate investing. Cultivate a mindset that embraces change and remains open to new strategies and ideas.

The key to investing in a changing economy lies in adaptability, resilience, and the willingness to learn. By incorporating these principles into your investment strategy, you'll be better equipped to navigate the highs and lows of the market and unlock the secrets to success in real estate investing. As Armando once wisely told me, "The economy is like the seasons, and the savvy investor knows how to make the most of each one."

Remember that both caution and calculated risks are essential elements in your real estate journey. By finding the balance between the wisdom of Armando and the careful guidance of my mother, I've managed to build a profitable and enduring investment portfolio. Embrace the ever- hanging nature of the economy and use it as an opportunity to grow and succeed in the world of real estate investing.

Chapter 37

The Future of Real Estate

I recall a conversation I had with one of my mentors, Armando, many years ago. We were sitting in his office, As he discussed the ever changing landscape of real estate, he then said, "The future of real estate will be shaped by those who can adapt, innovate, and embrace the changes that come their way."

His words have resonated with me throughout my journey in real estate investing. The future is uncertain, but with the right mindset and approach, one can thrive in this constantly evolving industry.

In this chapter, I'll share my thoughts on the future of real estate and some essential strategies for navigating the uncharted waters ahead.

One of the most significant changes in the real estate industry in recent years has been the rise of technology. From virtual tours and digital transactions to artificial intelligence and big data, technology is transforming the way we buy, sell, and manage properties.

As a real estate investor, it's crucial to stay informed about emerging technologies and adapt them to your advantage. For instance, leveraging online platforms for property listings, research, and networking can give you a competitive edge in the market.

Furthermore, staying up to date with technological advancements will allow you to anticipate and adapt to new trends, ultimately increasing the efficiency and profitability of your investments.

Another trend shaping the future of real estate is the increasing emphasis on sustainability. More and more people are becoming environmentally conscious, which is reflected in their preferences for eco-friendly homes and communities.

As an investor, it's essential to consider the long term value of sustainable features in your properties. By incorporating energy efficient appliances, solar panels, or green construction materials, you can attract environmentally conscious tenants and buyers, while also potentially reducing operating costs and increasing property value.

The world's population is becoming increasingly urbanized, with more people moving to cities in search of job opportunities and a better quality of life. This trend has significant implications for real estate investors.

As cities continue to grow, the demand for affordable housing, mixed use developments, and innovative living solutions will increase. Investors who can identify these opportunities and develop properties that cater to the evolving needs of urban dwellers will be well positioned for success in the future.

Additionally, shifting demographics, such as an aging population and a growing number of remote workers, will impact the types of properties in demand. Staying attuned to these changes and adjusting your investment strategy accordingly will be essential for long term success.

As Armando so wisely advised, the future of real estate lies in the hands of those who can adapt, innovate, and embrace change. The ability to anticipate and adjust to market trends, new technologies, and evolving consumer preferences will be critical for successful investors in the years to come.

In the ever changing world of real estate, economic uncertainty is inevitable. However, successful investors understand the importance of resilience and flexibility when facing challenging market conditions.

In times of economic turmoil, it's essential to adopt a long term perspective and avoid making impulsive decisions based on short term fluctuations. By focusing on the fundamentals such as cash flow, property location, and quality you can weather economic storms and emerge stronger when conditions improve.

Finally, the future of real estate investing lies in the hands of those who are committed to lifelong learning and continuous improvement. As the industry evolves, so must your knowledge and skills.

Invest in your education by attending seminars, reading books, and seeking mentorship from experienced investors. Embrace new strategies and techniques, and be willing to step out of your comfort zone to explore uncharted territories in the world of real estate investing.

As I reflect on my journey in real estate investing, I'm reminded of the wisdom that Armando shared with me many years ago. The future of real estate is indeed shaped by those who can adapt, innovate, and embrace the changes that come their way.

While the path ahead may be filled with uncertainties and challenges, the opportunities for growth and success are boundless for those who dare to dream, learn, and evolve.

Embrace the future of real estate with an open mind and a resilient spirit, and you'll uncover the secrets that they don't want you to know.

Chapter 38

Scaling Your Real Estate Business

It was a Monday afternoon, as I was driving around the north east side of San Antonio inspecting my properties, I received a call from my friend and mentor, Tom. He was in town and wanted to catch up over lunch. I gladly accepted his invitation, eager to discuss my recent successes in the world of real estate investing.

As we sat down at a local taco restaurant, Tom asked me about my progress and how my investments were faring. I enthusiastically shared the details of my growing portfolio, and he listened attentively, nodding in approval.

After a moment of reflection, Tom looked me in the eye and said, "It's time to scale your business." I was intrigued by his suggestion but uncertain about the path forward. Sensing my hesitation, he proceeded to share invaluable insights that would transform my real estate investing journey.

Tom's advice on scaling my real estate business revolved around seven key strategies:

Build a strong foundation. To successfully scale your real estate business, you must first ensure that you have a solid foundation. This means honing your skills, understanding market trends, and mastering the art of deal-making. Only when you have a firm grasp of the fundamentals can you confidently expand your portfolio and take on more significant projects.

Develop a growth mindset. Scaling a real estate business requires an unwavering belief in your ability to grow and succeed. Tom emphasized the importance of a growth mindset, urging me to challenge my self-imposed limitations and embrace the idea that I could achieve even greater heights.

By cultivating a growth mindset, you'll be better equipped to tackle obstacles, learn from your mistakes, and seize opportunities to expand your business.

Systematize and delegate. As your real estate business grows, managing every aspect of your investments can become increasingly challenging. Tom recommended that I create systems to streamline my processes and delegate tasks to competent professionals.

Hiring a property manager, for example, can alleviate the burden of day to day management and allow you to focus on more strategic aspects of your business. Similarly, enlisting the help of a real estate agent or an accountant can free up your time to scout for new deals and explore innovative investment strategies.

Diversify your portfolio. Scaling your real estate business doesn't just mean acquiring more properties; it also involves diversifying your portfolio to minimize risk and maximize returns. Tom encouraged me to explore different types of properties, such as commercial real estate, vacation rentals, or multi-family dwellings.

By diversifying your investments, you can mitigate the impact of market fluctuations and create multiple income streams to support your growing business.

Leverage your network. Tom emphasized the importance of leveraging my network to support my expansion efforts. He reminded me that real estate is a relationship-driven business, and my connections with fellow investors, agents, and industry professionals could be instrumental in my growth.

By nurturing relationships, attending networking events, and collaborating with like-minded individuals, I could access new opportunities and gain valuable insights to fuel my business's growth.

Invest in education. Continuing education is crucial for staying ahead of the curve in the real estate industry. Tom urged me to invest in my knowledge by attending seminars, workshops, and courses that would help me become a better investor.

By constantly learning and staying up to date with the latest trends and strategies, I would be better equipped to identify and capitalize on new opportunities for growth.

Focus on long-term goals. Finally, Tom stressed the importance of maintaining a long term perspective when scaling my real estate business. Rather than getting caught up in short term gains, I should set clear, long term goals for my business and work diligently to achieve them.

By focusing on the bigger picture and measuring my progress against my long-term objectives, I could ensure steady and sustainable growth for my business for years to come.

As our lunch came to an end, I thanked Tom for his invaluable advice and vowed to implement his strategies in my real estate investing journey.

Today, as I look back on that pivotal conversation, I'm grateful for Tom's guidance and the lessons he shared. By following his advice and embracing the challenge of scaling my real estate business, I've unlocked new levels of success and uncovered even more secrets they don't want you to know.

The journey of scaling a real estate business is undoubtedly filled with challenges and uncertainties, but it's also a path that leads to immense rewards and fulfillment. By applying these seven strategies and staying committed to your goals, you can navigate the complexities of growth and achieve lasting success in the world of real estate investing.

Chapter 39

Overcoming Challenges and Obstacles

There I was, packing my bags into my car, feeling a mixture of excitement and nervousness. With only $900 to my name, I left my hometown of El Paso, embarking on a journey that would shape my life and teach me invaluable lessons. As I drove towards San Antonio, I knew that overcoming challenges and obstacles would become a cornerstone of my success in this new journey.

When I arrived in San Antonio, my friend Robert opened his home to me, allowing me to sleep on his couch while I found my footing in this unfamiliar city. It was during this time, living on Robert's couch, that I realized the importance of resilience and adaptability in the face of adversity.

This period of my life taught me that facing challenges head-on was critical for my growth as a real estate investor.

I quickly learned that the key to success in this competitive industry was having the ability to adapt to change and overcome obstacles.

As I ventured further into the world of real estate investing, I faced numerous challenges. I had to learn the intricacies of the local market, network with industry professionals, and acquire the necessary skills and knowledge to succeed. Each challenge I overcame brought me one step closer to uncovering the secrets they don't want you to know.

One of the most significant obstacles I faced was finding my niche in the real estate market. I experimented with various property types, strategies, and markets until I discovered the right fit for my unique skill set and goals. This process of trial and error was crucial for developing the resilience and resourcefulness required to succeed in this competitive industry.

Another challenge I faced was building a strong network in a new city. I had to step outside my comfort zone, attend networking events, and foster meaningful relationships with fellow investors, agents, and industry professionals. By overcoming this obstacle, I unlocked new opportunities and gained valuable insights that contributed to my success.

Education also played a vital role in overcoming challenges and obstacles in my real estate journey. By attending seminars, workshops, and courses, I was able to stay ahead of the curve and adapt to the ever changing landscape of the real estate market.

As I reflect on my journey from sleeping on Robert's couch in San Antonio to becoming a successful real estate investor, I am reminded of the power of determination, resilience, and an unwavering belief in oneself.

Overcoming challenges and obstacles is one of the secrets they don't want you to know about, but it is integral to your success as a real estate investor. By embracing adversity and learning to adapt, you can develop the skills and mindset necessary to thrive in this competitive industry.

As you continue on your real estate investing journey, remember that every challenge and obstacle you face is an opportunity for growth. Embrace these experiences, learn from them, and use them as stepping stones towards unlocking the secrets of real estate success they don't want you to know.

Chapter 40

Overcoming Fear and Procrastination

Life is full of moments where we must make a choice: to face our fears and take a leap of faith, or to let fear hold us back and continue living in our comfort zone. As a real estate investor, I've learned that overcoming fear and procrastination is one of the secrets they don't want you to know, and it's a key to unlocking success.

It was during my friend and fellow real estate investor Carlos's wife's birthday celebration that I had one of those life changing moments. As I entered the lively party, I noticed a beautiful woman named Jessica, sitting down and having a conversation with her sister. My heart raced, and I knew I had to overcome my fear and seize the opportunity to introduce myself.

With a deep breath, I mustered the courage to interrupt their conversation and asked Jessica to dance. In that moment, as we danced and laughed together, I fell in love with her and knew she was the one for me. This experience taught me that overcoming fear and taking action can lead to incredible rewards, both personally and professionally.

In the world of real estate investing, overcoming fear and procrastination is essential for success. Much like for me it was approaching my wife Jessica at that party, real estate investors must face their fears head on and take action, even when it feels uncomfortable or uncertain.

Fear can manifest in many ways in real estate investing, such as the fear of failure, the fear of taking on too much risk, or the fear of making a poor investment decision. Procrastination, on the other hand, can stem from feelings of overwhelm, analysis paralysis, or simply the lack of motivation.

To overcome fear and procrastination, consider these strategies:

Set clear and attainable goals: By setting realistic goals and breaking them down into smaller, manageable steps, you can focus on taking consistent action, which helps to alleviate fear and procrastination.

Educate yourself: Gaining knowledge and expertise in your chosen field can help reduce fear and uncertainty. By becoming more knowledgeable about real estate investing, you can make more informed decisions and build confidence in your abilities.

Surround yourself with like-minded individuals: Having a supportive network of peers, mentors, and fellow investors can provide encouragement and guidance when facing fear and procrastination. Their experiences and insights can help you navigate challenging situations and stay accountable to your goals.

Embrace failure as a learning opportunity: By accepting that failure is a natural part of the learning process, you can view setbacks as opportunities to grow and improve, rather than as reasons to avoid taking action.

Practice mindfulness and self-compassion: Cultivating mindfulness and self-compassion can help you face your fears with a kinder, more understanding attitude. This approach allows you to acknowledge your fears without being paralyzed by them and encourages you to take action in spite of them.

As a real estate investor, overcoming fear and procrastination is an essential skill that can lead to greater success and fulfillment. Just as I faced my fears and approached my wife Jessica at the party, you can face your fears in real estate investing and discover the incredible opportunities that await you.

Remember, one of the secrets they don't want you to know is that overcoming fear and procrastination is crucial for achieving success in real estate investing. Embrace these challenges and seize the opportunities that come your way, and you'll unlock the doors to a brighter and more prosperous future.

Chapter 41

Your Ego is Not Your Amigo

As I began to find success in the world of real estate investing, I couldn't help but feel a sense of pride and accomplishment. After all, I had worked hard to build my skills and knowledge, and I was finally reaping the rewards of my efforts. However, it didn't take long for my growing ego to cast a shadow over my achievements.

One day, while discussing my recent successes with my friend and mentor, Tom, I found myself bragging about the great deals I had closed and the money I was making. Tom listened patiently, but then he stopped me and said something that would forever change my perspective: "Alberto, your ego is not your amigo."

His words hit me like a ton of bricks. I realized that my ego had started to take over, leading me to become arrogant and overconfident. I knew that if I wanted to continue growing as a real estate investor, I would need to keep my ego in check.

Tom went on to explain that in the world of real estate investing, humility and self awareness are essential traits. By acknowledging our strengths and weaknesses, we can make better decisions, learn from our mistakes, and continue to grow as investors. He shared that one of the secrets they don't want you to know is that a balanced ego can be the key to long-term success.

I took Tom's advice to heart and began to actively work on managing my ego. I learned that a healthy ego can help us stay confident and motivated, while an overinflated ego can lead to poor decision-making and a lack of growth. Here are some strategies I used to keep my ego in check:

Stay humble and grateful: Remember that no matter how much success you achieve, there is always more to learn. Be grateful for your accomplishments, but also recognize the role that luck, timing, and the support of others have played in your success.

Seek feedback and be open to criticism: Actively seek out feedback from others, even if it's difficult to hear. Be open to criticism and use it as an opportunity to learn and improve.

Embrace learning and growth: Acknowledge that you don't know everything and commit to continuous learning. Stay curious and open-minded, and embrace new ideas and perspectives.

Surround yourself with diverse perspectives: Engage with people who have different backgrounds, experiences, and opinions. This can help to challenge your assumptions and prevent you from becoming complacent in your thinking.

Reflect on your actions and decisions: Regularly take the time to reflect on your actions and decisions. Consider how your ego may have influenced your choices and identify areas where you can improve.

By implementing these strategies, I was able to keep my ego in check and continue to grow as a real estate investor. As Tom taught me, your ego is not your amigo, and managing it is an essential aspect of achieving long term success in the world of real estate investing.

Learning to manage my ego was a transformative experience that helped me become a more effective and successful real estate investor. By adopting a humble and growth oriented mindset, I was able to build stronger relationships, make better decisions, and stay resilient in the face of challenges.

As I continued on my journey as a real estate investor, I began to notice the impact that managing my ego had on my relationships and decision making. By keeping my ego in check, I found that I was more open to collaboration and willing to learn from others. This, in turn, helped me to build a stronger network of contacts and form more valuable partnerships.

Remember, one of the secrets they don't want you to know is that keeping your ego in check is vital for achieving long term success in real estate investing. Embrace humility, open-mindedness, and continuous learning, and you'll be well on your way to building a thriving real estate business that stands the test of time.

Chapter 42

The Power of Networking

A s my real estate investing journey progressed, I came to understand the importance of building a strong network. I had learned the value of managing my ego, and I knew that I couldn't do everything on my own. It was during this period that I discovered the power of networking, which would become a crucial part of my success in real estate.

I began attending seminars, workshops, and live events, eager to learn from experienced investors and professionals in the industry. At these events, I not only gained valuable knowledge, but I also started building connections with people who would prove to be invaluable assets in my real estate career.

One of the greatest benefits of networking I experienced was the ability to leverage other people's resources, commonly known as OPM (Other People's Money), OPE (Other People's Experience), and OPT (Other People's

Time). By tapping into these resources, I was able to scale my real estate business much faster than if I had tried to do it all on my own.

For example, through networking, I met a seasoned investor named Eduardo who had a wealth of experience and capital to invest. He was interested in partnering with me on a few deals, and as a result, I was able to use his money (OPM) to finance the projects without having to come up with the entire investment myself.

Similarly, I connected with Nicole, a property manager with years of experience managing rental properties. She shared her knowledge and expertise (OPE) with me, helping me avoid common pitfalls and ensure my properties were managed efficiently and effectively. This partnership saved me countless hours of trial and error, allowing me to focus on growing my business.

Finally, I met Luis, a contractor who had a team of skilled professionals working with him. By leveraging his team's time (OPT), I was able to complete renovations and repairs on my properties much faster than if I had tried to do it all myself.

These connections and many others I made through networking proved to be invaluable in my real estate journey. The power of networking is one of the secrets they don't want you to know, as it can significantly impact your success as a real estate investor.

To fully harness the power of networking, remember to:

Attend industry events: Seminars, workshops, and conferences are great places to meet like-minded professionals and learn from their experiences.

Be genuine and authentic: When networking, focus on building real connections with people, rather than just trying to collect business cards.

Offer value to others: Share your own knowledge and expertise with others, and they will be more likely to reciprocate.

Stay in touch: Follow up with the contacts you make and nurture those relationships over time.

Be open to collaboration: Realize that you don't have to do everything on your own and that partnering with others can lead to even greater success.

By embracing the power of networking, you can unlock new opportunities, access valuable resources, and grow your real estate business faster than you ever thought possible. Remember, this is one of the secrets they don't want you to know, but it's essential for long-term success in real estate investing.

Chapter 43

Real Estate Seminars and Education

As I progressed in my real estate investing journey, I quickly realized that knowledge was one of the most powerful tools I could possess. The more I learned, the more opportunities I saw, and the more confident I became in my decision-making. This is when I began to understand the importance of real estate seminars and education.

I had heard about these seminars and workshops from some of my connections, and I decided to invest in myself by attending as many as I could. I knew that by learning from others who had already walked the path I was on, I could compress time and avoid many of the mistakes that they had made.

One of the first seminars I attended was led by a successful real estate investor named James. He shared his insights and experiences, offering invaluable advice to those of us who were just starting. It was through his seminar that I connected with my first real estate mentor, who would later become a significant influence on my career.

My mentor, Armando, had years of experience in real estate investing and had encountered many of the challenges I was facing. He was able to guide me through the process, helping me to identify potential pitfalls and minimize my risks. By learning from his experiences (OPE), I was able to make better decisions and achieve success more quickly than if I had tried to navigate the journey alone.

As I continued to attend seminars and workshops, I discovered the value of engaging with the other participants. I would often stay late after the sessions, discussing real estate strategies and exchanging ideas with my fellow attendees. These conversations led to the formation of new friendships, as well as potential business partnerships. I also gained insights into various markets and niches, which helped me broaden my perspective as an investor.

In addition to the formal seminars, I began to seek out other educational resources, such as books, podcasts, and online courses. I found that learning from multiple sources allowed me to gain a more comprehensive understanding of the real estate industry. Each resource provided a different perspective, and by absorbing as much information as possible, I could see the bigger picture and make more informed decisions.

The impact of real estate seminars and education on my life cannot be overstated. I truly believe that the knowledge and connections I gained through these experiences played a crucial role in my success as a real estate investor. Furthermore, I firmly believe that anyone who is serious about achieving success in real estate investing should make a commitment to their own education and personal development.

Here's why real estate seminars and education are essential for investors:

Gain valuable knowledge: Learning from experts in the field can help you make informed decisions and minimize risks in your investments.

Build your network: Attending seminars and workshops is an excellent way to meet like-minded individuals who can become valuable contacts and potential partners.

Learn from others' experiences (OPE): Save time and avoid costly mistakes by learning from those who have already encountered the challenges you may face.

Stay up to date with industry trends: Real estate is an ever-changing field, and it's essential to stay informed about new strategies and techniques.

Enhance your skills: Continuous education allows you to develop and refine the skills necessary for success in real estate investing.

Real estate seminars and education are one of the secrets they don't want you to know. By investing in yourself and taking advantage of these learning opportunities, you can increase your chances of success and create a more prosperous future in real estate investing. Embrace the power of knowledge and watch as your real estate business flourishes.

The journey to success in real estate investing is filled with challenges and obstacles. However, with the right mindset, dedication, and the willingness to learn and grow, you can overcome these barriers and achieve your goals. By attending real estate seminars and furthering your education, you can acquire the skills, knowledge, and connections necessary to thrive in this competitive industry.

Never underestimate the importance of continuous learning and self-improvement. As the saying goes, knowledge is power, and in the world of real estate investing, it can be the difference between success and failure. So, attend seminars, read books, listen to podcasts, and engage with others in the industry to expand your knowledge and stay ahead of the curve.

Remember, the secrets to success in real estate investing are often hidden in plain sight. By embracing these opportunities for growth and development, you can unlock your full potential and create a prosperous future in the world of real estate. So, take that leap of faith, invest in yourself, and watch as your dreams become a reality.

Chapter 44

Real Estate Books and Resources

I still remember the first time I picked up a book about real estate investing. It was a worn, old copy of a classic that I found at a local bookstore. The pages were yellowed, and the cover had seen better days, but that didn't matter to me. I was captivated by the idea of creating wealth through real estate and was eager to learn all I could.

As I flipped through the pages, I couldn't help but feel a sense of excitement building within me. The author's words spoke to me, igniting a fire that would ultimately lead me to become a successful real estate investor. It was through books like this one that I learned the ins and outs of the industry, from finding deals and negotiating contracts to managing properties and tenants.

In the years that followed, I continued to devour every real estate book I could get my hands on. I read about the successes and failures of other investors, learning from their experiences and adapting their strategies to suit my own goals and circumstances. I also made a point to stay up-to-date with the latest industry trends and news, subscribing to newsletters and following influential blogs.

The importance of real estate books and resources cannot be overstated. As an investor, you must constantly strive to expand your knowledge and stay informed about the ever-changing world of real estate. It's through this continuous learning process that you can stay ahead of the curve and make the most informed decisions possible.

One of the secrets they don't want you to know is just how vital these resources are in the journey to real estate success. By leveraging the wisdom and experience of others, you can compress time and accelerate your path to achieving your goals. And in an industry as competitive as real estate, every advantage you can gain is crucial.

Here are some reasons why real estate books and resources are essential for investors:

Build a strong foundation: Reading books on real estate investing can help you understand the basic principles and strategies that will guide your investment decisions.

Learn from the best: Many successful real estate investors have shared their experiences and insights through books and articles, providing invaluable lessons for those just starting out.

Stay up-to-date on industry trends: Real estate is a constantly evolving field, and staying informed about the latest developments can give you an edge in the market.

Find inspiration and motivation: Reading about the successes of other real estate investors can inspire and motivate you to keep pushing forward in your own journey.

Develop your skills: By continuously learning and applying new knowledge, you can hone your skills and become a more effective and efficient real estate investor.

If you're serious about achieving success in the world of real estate investing, you must make a commitment to your education and personal development. By reading books, following blogs, and engaging with other investors, you can build a wealth of knowledge that will serve you well in your journey.

The truth is, real estate investing is a multifaceted field, and no single book or resource can cover every aspect of it. That's why it's essential to diversify your sources of information and continually seek new opportunities to learn and grow. By doing so, you'll be better equipped to face the challenges that arise in your real estate career and ultimately achieve your goals.

The road to real estate success is paved with a wealth of resources just waiting to be tapped into. From books and articles to podcasts, webinars, and networking events, there's a virtually endless supply of information at your fingertips. The key is to be proactive in seeking out these resources, embracing the lessons they offer, and applying them to your unique journey as a real estate investor.

So take the time to invest in yourself and your education. Seek out the best real estate books and resources available and make it a priority to learn something new every day, don't be content with just reading a single book or attending a single seminar. With this mindset and dedication to continuous learning, you'll be well on your way to unlocking the secrets of real estate investing and achieving the success you've always dreamed of.

Chapter 45

The Power of Generational Wealth

As my journey into real estate investing progressed, I started to understand that it was about more than just accumulating wealth for myself. I realized that the true power of real estate investing lay in its capacity to create generational wealth–a legacy that could be passed down to future generations of my family.

One day, while attending a real estate seminar, I had the pleasure of listening to a successful real estate investor share his story. He was a third-generation real estate investor, and his family had been building and managing a vast portfolio of properties for over a century. The impact of their investments extended far beyond their immediate family, providing jobs, housing, and opportunities for countless individuals in their community.

This family's story struck a chord with me, as it demonstrated the power of generational wealth and the potential it had to not only change my life but the lives of my future descendants and those around me. I realized that by strategically investing in real estate, I could create a legacy that would benefit my family for generations to come–even though I didn't have children yet, I knew this was something I wanted to work towards.

Inspired by this newfound understanding, I began to think bigger in terms of my investment strategies. I started to look for opportunities that would not only generate income but also provide long-term value and growth potential. I focused on acquiring properties that would not only appreciate in value but also serve as a stable source of income for my future family.

As my real estate portfolio grew, I began to see the tangible impact of my investments on my own financial security, moreover, I was building a foundation for future generations, ensuring that they would have the resources they needed to pursue their dreams and continue the legacy I had started.

The idea of generational wealth also made me reflect on the importance of financial education. I understood that, to truly create a lasting legacy, I needed to pass on not only my assets but also my knowledge and experience in real estate investing. I began to educate myself more rigorously, attending seminars, reading books, and connecting with other successful investors. This way, when the time came for me to pass on my legacy, my future children and grandchildren would be well-equipped to manage and grow the wealth I had built.

I also realized that the power of generational wealth extended beyond the financial benefits it provided. It also offered a sense of pride and accomplishment, knowing that the hard work, dedication, and smart decisions made today would have a lasting impact on the lives of those who come after us. It's a powerful motivator that drives me to continue pushing the boundaries of what's possible in real estate investing and to never stop learning and growing.

As I look to the future, I'm excited by the possibilities that lie ahead. I know that by continuing to invest in real estate and prioritizing generational wealth, I'm not only securing my own financial future but also creating a lasting legacy for my family.

The power of generational wealth is one of the most profound secrets of real estate investing. It's a game-changer that can transform not only your own life but the lives of those who come after you. By embracing this mindset and focusing on creating a lasting legacy through real estate, you can unlock the true potential of this incredible wealth-building tool and change the course of your family's history forever. As you venture forth into the world of real estate investing, remember the power that lies in building generational wealth, and let it guide you towards a brighter, more prosperous future.

As you continue to read and learn from this book, always remember the importance of creating a lasting legacy for your family and the impact it can have on future generations. Keep the lessons you've learned in mind as you venture into the world of real estate investing and strive to create generational wealth for yourself and those who come after you.

Remember that the secrets shared in this book are here to guide you on your journey, and with persistence and dedication, you can achieve incredible success in real estate investing.

Chapter 46

Be a Ghost

One normal afternoon, I was having lunch with my friend and fellow real estate investor, Carlos. As we enjoyed our meal and discussed our latest investments, Carlos leaned in and said, "Alberto, I want to share something with you, something I've never told anyone before. The most important secret of my success in real estate." Intrigued, I listened closely as Carlos proceeded to share his secret: "Be a Ghost."

I was puzzled at first, but Carlos went on to explain that being a "ghost" in the world of real estate meant protecting your wealth by carefully allocating your assets using the right legal structures and financial strategies. To truly become successful and protect your hard-earned investments, you need to be invisible, like a ghost.

Carlos shared that the key to becoming a ghost was to have a strong team of professionals behind you. This team should include corporate lawyers, trust attorneys, accountants who understand the strategies of the top one percent, and other experts who can help you navigate the complex world of asset protection.

He explained that by using corporations, trusts, and umbrella insurance policies, you can effectively separate yourself from your assets, making it harder for anyone to come after your wealth. Essentially, you don't own anything, but you control everything.

To illustrate his point, Carlos told me about one of his properties, a beautiful house worth $400,000 that he had recently paid off in full. He had set up a separate entity, which he also controlled, and placed a lien against the house for $500,000. On paper, the house appeared to have negative equity, discouraging any potential lawsuits or creditors from trying to seize the property.

I was amazed at Carlos's strategy and realized that this was one of the secrets they don't want you to know about. Being a ghost was a powerful way to protect your wealth and ensure that you could continue to build your real estate empire without the fear of losing it all.

Over the years, I've learned more about the art of being a ghost and have incorporated these strategies into my own real estate investing journey. I've set up corporations and trusts, and I've worked with top-notch professionals to ensure that my wealth is protected. I've learned that being a ghost is not just about hiding your assets, but also about taking control of your financial future.

So, as you continue to grow and learn in the world of real estate, remember the power of being a ghost. By understanding the importance of asset protection and working with a team of professionals who can help you navigate this complex world, you can build a successful real estate empire and protect your hard-earned wealth.

Embrace the secret of being a ghost, and let it guide you on your journey to real estate success.

The journey to real estate success is filled with secrets that only a select few are willing to share. One of the most important secrets I've learned throughout my journey is the power of being a ghost. By understanding the importance of asset protection and working with a strong team of professionals, you can shield your wealth and keep it safe from potential threats.

As you continue on your path to real estate success, always remember the lessons you've learned from this book, including the secret of being a ghost. By applying these strategies and tips, you'll be well on your way to building a lasting legacy and creating generational wealth for you and your family.

Remember, real estate is a powerful tool for building wealth and financial freedom. But to truly succeed, you must be willing to learn, adapt, and grow. Keep pushing forward, stay curious, and never stop seeking knowledge. The secrets you uncover may just be the key to unlocking the life of your dreams.

Chapter 47

Giving Back and Creating a Legacy

Throughout my journey in real estate, I've learned many valuable lessons that have shaped the person I am today. But none are as important as the lesson of giving back and creating a legacy. This final secret is one that I believe truly encompasses the spirit of success and the power of real estate investing.

I was once told, "You can't take it with you when you go." This simple phrase had a profound impact on me, and it has since become the driving force behind my desire to leave a lasting legacy for my family, my community, and the world at large. I've come to understand that success in real estate is not solely about accumulating wealth, but also about giving back and creating a legacy that will live on long after we're gone.

I believe that giving back is a universal law, much like gravity. We may not fully understand how it works, but we know it exists and has a powerful impact on our lives. Just as gravity always pulls objects toward the ground, giving back has a magnetic pull that attracts even more blessings and opportunities into our lives. It's a cycle of abundance that cannot be ignored.

As a real estate investor, I've had the privilege of acquiring wealth and knowledge that has changed my life for the better. But with this privilege comes responsibility - the responsibility to share my knowledge and resources with others, and to help those who are less fortunate.

I've learned that true success is not measured by the size of your bank account or the number of properties in your portfolio, but by the lives you touch and the difference you make in the world. By sharing the strategies and secrets I've learned throughout my journey, I hope to inspire others to give back and create their own legacy.

One of the most rewarding aspects of giving back is seeing the ripple effect it has on others. When we extend a helping hand, we not only improve the lives of those we help, but we also inspire them to do the same for others. This creates a cycle of giving that continues to grow and expand, impacting countless lives along the way.

As you continue to grow your real estate business and implement the strategies shared in the previous 46 chapters, I encourage you to keep the importance of giving back and creating a legacy in mind. Use your success and wealth to make a difference in the lives of others, and in doing so, you will find that your own life becomes even more fulfilling and meaningful.

The journey to real estate success is not a linear path, but a series of twists and turns filled with lessons, challenges, and opportunities for growth. By embracing the secrets shared in this book and living a life of abundance, you can unlock your full potential as a real estate investor and create a legacy that will last for generations to come.

As you continue to navigate the world of real estate investing, remember to always give back and help others along the way. By sharing your knowledge, resources, and time, you can create a positive impact on the lives of those around you and set an example for future generations.

Never forget that the true measure of success is not the wealth you accumulate, but the lives you touch and the legacy you leave behind. Keep this in mind as you continue to grow your real estate business, and you will find that the rewards and satisfaction of giving back far outweigh any financial gain.

Remember, the secrets to real estate success are not just about acquiring wealth, but also about using that wealth to give back and create a lasting legacy. By embracing this final secret and living a life of generosity, you'll not only achieve financial success, but you'll also experience the joy and fulfillment that comes from making a lasting impact on the world around you.

Chapter 48

Final Words

As I sit here reflecting on our journey together through the pages of "Basic Real Estate Secrets They Don't Want You to Know," I am filled with immense gratitude. Thank you for taking the time to read or listen to this book. It is my sincerest hope that you have gained valuable insights that will propel you forward in your real estate investing journey.

My only desire is that you take at least one thing from this book and use it to create positive change in your life. My goal is to help entrepreneurs become better entrepreneurs by sharing the real estate secrets they don't want you to know. Remember, knowledge is power, and with the right tools and mindset, you can achieve anything you set your mind to.

Now, I want to leave you with a bonus secret they don't want you to know: urgency. Let me ask you a question. Do you think it's possible for an entrepreneur to have $50,000 in one place at one time? Most likely, you answered yes. Now, do you think it's possible for the same entrepreneur to have 50,000 days to live on this planet? The answer is no.

The average human lives for 72 years - some live longer, some less - but 72 years times 365 five days equals only 26,280 days. And that's if you were born today! Time is our most precious asset, and we must use it wisely to achieve our dreams and leave a lasting legacy.

As you move forward in your real estate investing journey, always remember that every day is a gift. Embrace the opportunities that come your way and seize them with both hands. Build a strong foundation of knowledge, be open to learning from your experiences, and never be afraid to take risks.

Surround yourself with like-minded individuals who share your passion for real estate investing, and together, you will create a powerful force for change. Network, learn from others, and share your own experiences to help others grow and succeed.

So, as you close this book and embark on your real estate investing journey, I urge you to take massive action. Don't wait for the perfect moment, because it may never come. Start today, and make each day count. Break free from the limitations that have held you back, and step boldly into the future with determination and purpose.

And as you progress in your journey, remember to give back to others. Mentor those who are just starting, share your experiences, and help build a community of like minded investors. The more you give, the more you will receive. It's the law of the universe, and it works every time.

Also, don't forget the importance of building a legacy. What do you want to be remembered for? What impact will you have on the world? Use your success in real estate investing to create something meaningful that will stand the test of time. Whether it's through philanthropy, mentoring, or simply creating a better life for your family, always strive to leave a lasting, positive impact.

Stay connected with those who support your dreams and believe in your vision. Your network is your net worth, and together, you can achieve incredible things. Learn from each other, support each other, and celebrate each other's successes. As you grow and evolve as a real estate investor, your network will be the backbone of your continued growth and success.

Finally, never stop learning. The world of real estate investing is vast and ever changing. Stay curious, stay humble, and always be willing to learn something new. The more you learn, the more you'll grow, and the more successful you'll become. Invest in your education, read books, attend seminars, and seek out mentors who can guide you along your path. Knowledge is the key to unlocking the doors of opportunity, and with it, there are no limits to what you can achieve.

In closing, I want to express my deepest gratitude once again for joining me on this journey. It has been an honor to share my experiences and insights with you, and I hope they have inspired and empowered you to take action in your own life. Remember, the journey of a thousand miles begins with the first step. So, step out boldly into the world of real estate investing and create the life of your dreams.

And remember, As the great motivational speaker Les Brown once said, "You don't have to be great to get started, but you have to get started to be great."

I wish you all the best in your real estate journey and beyond. May you find success, fulfillment, and happiness in all that you do.

This is not the end, but rather a new beginning.

To be continued...

Sincerely,
Alberto Molina

BASIC REAL ESTATE
SECRETS
THEY DON'T WANT
YOU TO KNOW

ALBERTO MOLINA

www.ingramcontent.com/pod-product-compliance
Lightning Source LLC
Chambersburg PA
CBHW070330220526
45467CB00001B/105